The Black Man in America

SCOTT FORESMAN PROBLEMS IN AMERICAN HISTORY

General Editors: Edwin Fenton, *Carnegie-Mellon University*
David H. Fowler, *Carnegie-Mellon University*

THE BLACK MAN IN AMERICA

SECOND EDITION

LARRY CUBAN

Teacher and Administrator
Washington, D.C. Public Schools

SCOTT, FORESMAN

Historical Consultant:

Benjamin Quarles, Chairman

Department of History

Morgan State College, Baltimore, Maryland

COVER DESIGN BY ED BEDNO

Editors' Introduction

Growing numbers of history teachers realize that using source materials in their courses provides an added dimension of experience for their students. Total reliance on a textbook can no longer be considered an adequate means of learning history. Yet if the full value of documents and critical articles is to be obtained, they must be presented as something more than writings which record important events or as mere illustrations of what the text says. They must also challenge the student's ability to relate individual events to larger topics and to continuing themes in history.

Each volume of the SCOTT FORESMAN PROBLEMS IN AMERICAN HISTORY organizes source materials around one facet of our nation's past. A volume contains distinct Problems, each designed for one day's work. In some volumes the Problems are intended to be read individually, at the proper chronological intervals. In others, the Problems are grouped into units, each being best used as an uninterrupted week's work. Whether the Problems are studied individually or in units, they should be assigned only after the student has read the relevant material in his textbook.

One of the most vital services a collection of source materials can perform is to encourage the student to develop his critical abilities to the utmost in constructing historical explanations. Interpretation is the heart of history; the student should be brought to realize how essential it is to be able to do more with facts than memorize them. The SCOTT FORESMAN PROBLEMS are specifically designed to engage the student in the fascinating task of interpreting American history. Through them he will gain the skills and the enjoyment which come from reaching insight and understanding as well as knowledge of history.

Each Problem begins with an introduction written by the author to place documents in their historical context and to link together the Problems in a volume. These introductions prepare the student to read intelligently by defining the scope of the Problem, suggesting its relationship to larger issues, and pointing out difficulties of interpretation so that he will not attempt the impossible in generalizing from limited evidence.

The study questions at the end of the introduction carry the student further in applying the historian's critical tools. He may be asked to try to judge the reliability of a document or the bias of a critic, to assess an historical interpretation in the light of his knowledge, or to reason from particulars to a general conclusion of his own. Properly used, the study questions help beginning students find out what is important in source materials; without them, students often do not know what they are supposed to do with the readings.

To obtain more from a Problem than simply answers to the author's questions, the student should first read the introduction and questions and then pause to review what he already knows about the subject. Then, keeping the central issues in mind, he should study the entire Problem, perhaps first skimming through it to see the relationship of the parts to the whole, and then reading it carefully and taking notes. He will then be ready to consider his answers to the study questions in preparation for class discussion.

The teacher can use the SCOTT FORESMAN PROBLEMS in several ways. A Problem can perhaps serve most effectively as the basis for discussion by an entire class, with the lesson organized around the study questions or other questions proposed by the teacher to develop new points of view. What seems most appropriate for discussion will always depend partly upon the textbook used in the course and partly upon the instructor's own style of teaching and command of the subject. Each teacher should structure the discussion around those issues which he thinks are most important, but he should take care to link a Problem to those which preceded and which follow it. These connecting links give the student the maximum opportunity to comprehend the theme of the volume. By treating a limited number of issues within each Problem, a teacher should be able to restrict discussion to one class period.

These volumes can be used in other ways. Many readings can serve as the basis for reports to the class by individual students. An entire volume, or a selection of Problems from a volume, may be used in preparing a controlled research paper; the three-unit volumes are especially suited to this purpose. The Problems may also be assigned as supplementary reading in those areas where text treatment is not extensive.

In the present volume, *The Black Man in America*, Larry Cuban presents an aspect of American history that has long been neglected in our schools. The fifteen Problems trace the history of the black man as slave and freeman. They set forth the contributions of the black man to American society, examine his leadership and his institutions, and explore his long and arduous battle for equal rights. Many of the readings are first-hand accounts in which the black man speaks of and for himself. Students who use this volume are certain to gain a fresh appreciation of the role in our history played by one tenth of our nation's citizens.

EDWIN FENTON
DAVID H. FOWLER

PUBLISHER'S NOTE: The readings in this volume show capitalization and spellings of words, as well as sentence punctuation, as they appear in the sources from which they were taken. Thus, in many of the readings, especially in those which appeared previous to 1900, words such as Negro, Southern, and Northern are often not capitalized, as they are according to Scott Foresman style, and as they are in this book in the Problem introductions and headnotes. Omissions from the original texts are shown by ellipses, and interpolations, supplied by the author or editors for clarity, appear in brackets.

Table of Contents

Author's Introduction

A black student of mine once angrily fired three questions at me: Why did the only pictures of Negroes in his American history text show slaves picking cotton? Why didn't the book mention his race after the Civil War? Why wasn't the word "Negro" even listed in the index? My answer was weak. I explained that racist views often crept into texts; I pointed out instances where the text perpetuated time-worn stereotypes; finally, I said that texts were often a generation behind the social thought of the day. His retort was quick and to the point: "Sounds like Jim Crow history to me!"

This volume of the Scott Foresman series is an effort to enlarge the student's understanding of the Negro's role in American history. The fifteen Problems in this volume trace the path of the Negro from the auction block to the brink of first-class citizenship.

One main thread unites the experiences of slaves, ex-slaves, Southern Negro farmers, and Northern city dwellers, and that is, American Negroes have struggled to win those rights enjoyed by whites and promised to all Americans in the Declaration of Independence and in the Constitution. The story of the Negro traces the tension between what the Negro wanted as a citizen and what white Americans often refused to give him. No one can doubt that many twentieth-century Americans have not embraced entirely the ideals of the Declaration of Independence. If they have, why the sit-ins, the Freedom Rides, the bus boycotts, and the mass demonstrations of the 1960's? For Negroes, the ideals fought for in the Revolutionary War by both black and white have not yet become working realities. This, then, is the historic theme of the Negro's role in American history: How to narrow the gap between what is the ideal and what is the actuality.

Consider the demands of the mass of Negroes throughout history. They never advocated the violent overthrow of the American government. They never supported communism, socialism, or any other "ism." They never demanded the removal of Negroes from America to another land. Of course, a few American Negroes did leave the United States for Africa, and some others joined the Communist party. By and large, however, Negroes demanded only that full share of freedom and equality guaranteed them by the Constitution.

While the history of the black man in America is a sad tale, full of sorrow and bitterness, it has within it the seeds of a glorious future. If all Americans come to embrace sincerely the ideals of the Declaration of Independence, the black man will at last become a first-class citizen. The black "revolution" of the 1960's awakened America's social conscience. The difficult changes occurring in our lifetime are narrowing the gap between hope and realization. The final closing of that gap will signal the birth of a finer and better democracy. This volume traces the struggle, records the sorrow, and examines the seeds.

LARRY CUBAN

The author wishes to thank Professor G. Franklin Edwards of Howard University for assistance with Problem 11, "Class Structure in the Negro Community."

PROBLEM 1

The Origin of Slavery

A teacher asked his American history class why the Negro was enslaved. Some answers were: "Negroes didn't love freedom so much as Indians did." "Negroes were not so intelligent as whites." These answers represent unproved assumptions people have used to explain the enslavement of the Negro. Information about the role of the Negro during the colonial period will help destroy these myths and suggest better answers to this difficult question.

Fundamentally, slavery and other forms of bondage in colonial America existed for one reason: to fulfill the need for a cheap, reliable supply of labor. Land had to be cleared; crops had to be planted and cultivated; towns had to be built. From England and Europe came men, women, and children, contracted to work for several years, in payment for their passage or for some other reason. These indentured servants were an unreliable source of labor, however. Once their contracts were fulfilled, they left the farms and became landowners themselves or worked as skilled craftsmen. In some parts of the Americas, Indians were put to work on plantations, but when Negroes were brought to the colonies from Africa, they were preferred as laborers to the Indians. The differences in the cultures of the Indian and of the African help explain why Negroes adjusted to slavery and Indians did not.

Most Indians were hunters who wandered through the forest in search of game. The men of the tribe hunted and fought; they would not soil their hands with "squaw work," such as gathering fruits or cleaning killed game. Since Indians moved from place to place, they accumulated few possessions. Division of labor was almost unknown among the tribes, nor were Indians accustomed to taking and keeping slaves to do the heavy work.

African Negroes came from a more advanced culture. They lived in settled towns and in some cases in large cities. Most of their food was raised in nearby fields which the men prepared for tilling and the women cared for once the heavy labor was finished. In Africa, as in most advanced cultures, the men were not ashamed to work. Settled in villages or cities, the African could afford to accumulate possessions. Since the soil in many areas was rich, and agricultural techniques rather well advanced, some men could leave the farms to become craftsmen or artisans. Division of labor was highly developed. Moreover, the Africans were accustomed to having slaves about and lived with the knowledge that any man might become a slave. Thus, Negroes adjusted more easily to the culture of the American plantation than the Indian.

The first Africans who were brought to America, like the indentured servants who came under contract, were unfree for only a period of a few years—not for life. However, in 1664 the Maryland legislature ruled that Negroes must serve their masters for the rest of their lives. In 1669 a Virginia law stated that Negroes were property, but 1669 was a half century after "twenty Negars" stepped ashore at Jamestown, Virginia. These facts bring up an obvious question. If some whites, Africans, and Indians were in bondage in the first half of the seventeenth century, why did only Negroes become slaves for life?

Historians have not agreed upon an answer. Some believed that the heat, humidity, and agricultural crops of the South produced Negro slavery. Others stressed that Negro "inferiority" encouraged whites to enslave them and argued that Negroes were naturally docile and unintelligent. But the heat, humidity, and agricultural crops of the South after 1865 were identical to those before the Civil War. And certainly the numerous rebellions on slave ships did not reflect docility, nor did the perennial fear of a slave uprising on the plantations. Accomplishments of such Negroes as the poet Phillis Wheatley, the abolitionist Frederick Douglass, and the scientist Benjamin Banneker, who had opportunities to advance themselves, revealed the intelligence and talent latent within the Negro race. Today, historians have rejected these explanations. The answers suggested by Oscar and Mary Handlin and Carl N. Degler are presented in the readings for Problem 1. As you read, consider the following questions:

1   According to the Handlins, why was the Negro enslaved? Why was the Negro enslaved according to Degler? Which conclusion do you accept? Why?

2   Where do the Handlins and Degler agree in their arguments? Where do they disagree? Consider Degler's footnote.

3   Both Degler and the Handlins used basically the same information, yet they reach different conclusions. Why?

4   How important is it for us to know why the Negro was enslaved? Would race relations be improved if the reasons were known?

I

THE ECONOMIC ENVIRONMENT OF THE 1600'S

Oscar and Mary Handlin discuss the use of Negroes as laborers. □ From *Race and Nationality in American Life* by Oscar Handlin. Copyright 1948, 1950, 1953, © 1956, 1957, by Oscar Handlin. Reprinted by permission of Atlantic-Little, Brown and Co. and Collins-Knowlton-Wing, Inc. Pp. 7–28 passim.

Through the first three-quarters of the seventeenth century, the Negroes, even in the South, were not numerous; nor were they particularly concentrated in any district. They came into a society in which a large part of the population was to some degree unfree; indeed in Virginia under the Company almost everyone, even tenants and laborers, bore some sort of servile obligation. The Negroes' lack of freedom was not unusual. These newcomers, like so many others, were accepted, bought and held, as kinds of servants. They were certainly not well off. But their ill-fortune was of a sort they shared with men from England, Scotland, and Ireland, and with the unlucky aborigenes held in captivity. Like the others, some Negroes became free, that is, terminated their period of service. Some became artisans; a few became landowners and the masters of other men. The status of Negroes was that of servants; and so they were identified and treated down to the 1660's. . . .

Yet the Negroes did cease to be servants and became slaves, ceased to be men in whom masters held a proprietary interest and became chattels, objects that were the property of their owners. In that transformation originated the southern labor system.

Although the colonists assumed at the start that all servants would "fare alike in the colony," the social realities of their situation early gave rise to differences of treatment. . . . Like the millions who would follow, these immigrants longed in the strangeness for the company of familiar men and singled out . . . those who were most like themselves. So the measures regulating settlement spoke specifically in this period of differential treatment for various groups. From time to time, regulations applied only to "those of our own nation," or to the French, the Dutch, the Italians, the Swiss, . . . the Welsh, the Irish, or to combinations of the diverse nationalities. . . .

In the same way the colonists became aware of the differences between themselves and the African immigrants. The rudeness of the Negroes' manners, the strangeness of their languages, the difficulty of communicating to them English notions of morality and proper behavior occasioned sporadic laws to regulate their conduct. . . . Until the 1660's the statutes on the Negroes were not at all unique. Nor did they add up to a decided trend.

But in the decade after 1660 far more significant differentiations with regard to term of service, relationship to Christianity, and disposal of children, cut the Negro apart from all other servants and gave a new depth to his bondage. . . .

The question of length of service became critical when the mounting value of labor eased the fear that servants would be a drain on "vittles" and raised the expectation of profit from their toil. Those eager to multiply the number of available hands by stimulating immigration had not only to overcome the reluctance of a prospective newcomer faced with the trials of a sea journey; they had also to counteract the widespread reports in England and Scotland that servants were harshly treated and bound in perpetual slavery.

To encourage immigration therefore, the colonies embarked upon a line of legislation designed to improve servants' conditions and to enlarge the prospect of a meaningful release, a release that was not the start of a new period of servitude, but of life as a freeman and landowner. . . . These acts seem to have applied only to voluntary immigrants "of our own nation." The Irish and other aliens, less desirable, at first received longer terms. But the realization that such discrimination retarded "the peopling of the country" led to an extension of the identical privilege to all Christians.

But the Negro never profited from these enactments. . . . By midcentury the servitude of Negroes seems generally lengthier than that of whites; and thereafter the consciousness dawns that the Blacks will toil for the whole of their lives, not through any particular concern with their status but simply by contrast with those whose years of labor are limited by statute. . . .

But slavery for life was still tenuous as long as the slave could extricate himself by baptism. The fact that Negroes were heathens had formerly justified their bondage, since infidels were "perpetual" enemies of Christians. It had followed that conversion was a way to freedom. . . . As labor rose in value this presumption dissipated the zeal of masters for proselytizing. So that they be "freed from this doubt" a series of laws between 1667 and 1671 laid down the rule that conversion alone did not lead to a release from servitude.

Meanwhile the condition of the Negro deteriorated. In these very years, a startling growth in numbers complicated the problem. The Royal African Company was, to some extent, responsible, though its operations in the mainland colonies formed only a very minor part of its business. But the opening of Africa to free trade in 1698 inundated Virginia, Maryland, and South Carolina with new slaves. Under the pressure of policing these newcomers the regulation of Negroes actually grew harsher.

The early laws against runaways, against drunkenness, against carrying arms or trading without permission had applied penalties as heavy as death to all servants, Negroes and whites. But these regulations grew steadily less stringent in the case of white servants. On the other hand fear of the growing number of slaves, uneasy suspicion of plots and conspiracies, led to more stringent control of Negroes and a broad view of the master's power of discipline. Furthermore the emerging difference in treatment was calculated to create a real division of interest between Negroes on the one hand and whites on the other. . . .

. . . At the opening of the eighteenth century, the Black was not only set off by economic and legal status; he was "abominable," another order of man. . . .

Color then emerged as the token of the slave status; the trace of color became the trace of slavery. . . .

To this development there was a striking parallel in the northern colonies. For none of the elements that conspired to create the slave were peculiar to the productive system of the South. The contact of dissimilar peoples in an economy in which labor was short and opportunity long was common to all American settlements. In New England and New York too there had early been an intense desire for cheap unfree hands, for "bond slaverie, villinage or Captivitie," whether it be white, Negro, or Indian. As in the South, the growth in the number of Negroes had been slow until the end of the seventeenth century. The Negroes were servants who, like other bondsmen, became free and owners of land. But there too, police regulations, the rules of marriage, and the development of status as property turned them into chattel slaves.

A difference would emerge in the course of the eighteenth century, not so much in the cities . . . where there were substantial concentrations of Blacks, but in the rural districts where handfuls of Negroes were scattered under the easy oversight of town and church. There the slave would be treated as an individual, would become an equal, and acquire the rights of a human being. Men whose minds would be ever more preoccupied with conceptions of natural rights and personal dignity would find it difficult to except the Negro from their general rule.

But by the time the same preoccupations would fire imaginations in the South, the society in which the slave lived would so have changed that he would derive no advantage from the eighteenth-century speculations on the nature of human rights. Slavery had emerged in a society in which the unit of active agriculture was small and growing smaller; even the few large estates were operated by sub-division among tenants. After 1690, however, South Carolinians (and still later Georgians) turned from naval stores and the fur trade to the cultivation of rice, cotton, and indigo. In the production of these staples, which required substantial capital equipment, there was an advantage to large-scale operations. By then it was obvious which was the cheapest, most available, most exploitable labor supply. The immense profits from the tropical crops steadily sucked slaves in ever growing numbers into the plantation. With this extensive use, novel on the mainland, the price of slaves everywhere rose sharply, to the advantage of those who already held them. The prospect that the slaveowner would profit not only by the Negroes' labor, but also by the rise in their unit value and by their probable increase through breeding, accounted for the spread of the plantation to the older tobacco regions where large-scale production was not, as in the rice areas, necessarily an asset.

The new social and economic context impressed indelibly on the Negro the peculiar quality of chattel with which he had been left, as other servants escaped the general degradation that had originally been the common portion of all. . . .

The distinctive qualities of the southern labor system were then not the simple products of the plantation. They were rather the complex outcome of a process by which the American environment broke down the traditional European conceptions of servitude. In that process the weight of the plantation had pinned down on the Negro the clearly-defined status of a chattel, a status left him as other elements in the population achieved their liberation. When, therefore, Southerners in the eighteenth century came to think of the nature of the rights of man they found it inconceivable that Negroes should participate in those rights. It was more in accord with the whole social setting to argue that the slaves could not share those rights because they were not fully men, or [were] at least different kinds of men.

II

THE SOCIAL ATMOSPHERE OF THE 1600'S

Carl N. Degler discusses prejudices in the seventeenth century.   ☐ From *Out of Our Past* by Carl N. Degler, pp. 30–38. Copyright © 1959 by Carl N. Degler. Reprinted by permission of Harper & Row, Publishers, Incorporated.

American race prejudice originated in the discriminatory social atmosphere of the early seventeenth century, long before slavery came into legal existence. When slavery did become embodied in law, it could not help but reflect the folk bias within the framework of which it developed. Thus legal slavery in the English colonies reinforced and helped to perpetuate the discrimination against the Negro which prevailed almost from the beginning of settlement.

In the absence of restraining influences, it was not likely that men of the seventeenth century would accord Negroes an equal status with Englishmen. Even Irishmen, who were white, Christian, and European, were held to be literally "beyond the Pale" [or outcasts], and some were even referred to as "slaves." The African, after all, was a heathen at a time when "Christian" was a title of import; moreover, he was black and culturally different. . . . The fact that Negroes arrived in English America as the cargo of the international slave trade unquestionably fostered a sense of superiority among Englishmen. . . . It was to be anticipated that from the beginning a special inferior position would be assigned black men.

Such, indeed, was the fact even though the Virginia and Maryland records in the years between 1620 and 1660 rarely refer to "slaves" but speak mainly of "Negroes." . . . Moreover, the treatment accorded another dark-skinned heathen people, the Indians, offers further evidence that enslavement was early the lot reserved for Negroes. Indian slavery was practiced in all the English settlements almost from the beginning; rarely were any distinctions made between Indians and Negroes when discriminatory legislation was enacted. But let us now turn to the beginnings of slavery in the English colonies. . . .

There is evidence as early as the 1630's and 1640's that Virginia and Maryland were singling out Negroes for discriminatory treatment as compared with white indentured servants. . . . Negroes were specifically denied the right to bear arms in Virginia in 1640 and in Maryland in 1648, though no such prohibition was put upon white servants; indeed, in statutes that prohibited Negroes from being armed, masters were directed to arm the white servants. . . .

. . . Cases for the punishment of runaway servants in Virginia throw some light on the status of Negroes by 1640. . . .

[One] case . . . suggests that by that date some Negroes were already slaves. This one also involved six white men and a Negro who had plotted to run away. The punishments meted out varied, but Christopher Miller . . . was given the harshest treatment of all: thirty stripes, burned with an "R" (for Rogue) on the cheek, a shackle on his leg for a year "and longer if said master shall see cause," and seven years of service for the colony upon completion of his time due his master. The only other one of the plotters to receive the stripes, the shackle, and the burning of the "R" was the Negro Emanuel, but, significantly, he did not receive any sentence of work for the colony. Apparently he was already serving his master for a lifetime – i.e., he was a slave. . . .

In early seventeenth-century inventories of estates there are two distinctions which appear in the reckoning of the value of servants and Negroes. Uniformly, the Negroes are more valuable, even as children, than any white servant. Secondly, the naming of a servant is usually followed by the number of years yet remaining to his service; for the Negroes no such notation appears. Thus, in an inventory in Virginia in 1643, a twenty-two-year-old white servant, with eight years still to serve, was valued at 1,000 pounds of tobacco, while a "Negro boy" was rated at 3,000 pounds; a white boy with seven years to serve was listed as worth 700 pounds. An eight-year-old Negro girl was calculated to be worth 2,000 pounds. On another inventory in 1655, two good men servants with four years to serve were rated at 1,300 pounds of tobacco, and a woman servant with only two years to go was valued at 800 pounds. But two Negro boys, who had no limit set to their terms, were evaluated at 4,100 pounds apiece, and a Negro girl was said to be worth 5,500 pounds.

Such wide differences in the valuation of Negro and white "servants" strongly suggest, as does the failure to indicate term of service for Negroes, that the latter were slaves. . . .

More positive evidence of true slavery is afforded by the court records of the 1640's and 1650's. In 1646, for example, a Negro woman and a Negro boy were sold to Stephen Charlton to be of use to him and "his heyers etc. for ever." A Negro girl was sold in 1652 to one H. Armsteadinger "and his heyers . . . forever with all her increase both male and female." . . .

It is true that, concurrently with these examples of onerous service or actual slavery exacted from Negroes, some members of the race did gain their freedom. But such instances do not deny the existence of discrimination or slave status; they simply testify to the unsteady evolution of a status for the Negro. . . .

But as legal questions of status arose from time to time, clarification of the Negroes' position had to be written into law. Thus in 1662 Virginia declared that the status of offspring would follow that of the mother in the event of a white man getting a Negro with child. When Maryland in 1664 prescribed service for Negroes *durante vita* [for life] and included hereditary status through the *father*, it also prohibited unions between the races. The preamble of the statute offers a clue as to the motives behind this separation of the races. Prohibition of intermarriage is necessary because "divers free born *English* women, forgetful of their free condition, and to the disgrace of our nation, do intermarry with Negro slaves," from which fact questions of status of issue have arisen. Therefore, the law was enacted in order to prevent harm to masters and "for deterring such freeborn women from such shameful matches. . . ." Interestingly enough, the South Carolinian slave code of 1712 justified special legislation for Negroes on grounds of cultural difference. "The Negroes and other slaves brought unto the people of this province . . . are of barbarous, wild, savage natures, and such as renders them wholly unqualified to be governed by the laws, customs, and practices of this province. . . ."

The important point is not the evolution of the legal status of the slave, but the fact that discriminatory legislation regarding the Negro long preceded any legal definition of slavery. Equally important, in view of the commonly held view that numbers of Negroes determined the inferior status imposed upon the black, is the evidence of discrimination long before numbers were large. In 1680 Virginia enacted a series of regulations which were very close to the later slave codes in restricting the movement of Negroes, prohibiting their bearing arms, and providing capital punishment for those who ran away or offered resistance to whites. Yet it would be another twenty years before the Negroes would make up even a fifth of the total population of Virginia. In short, long before slavery was an important part of the labor system of the South, the Negroes had been fitted into a special and inferior status.

That the white man's sense of difference regarding the Negro determined the character of slavery is clearly seen if one examines the development of Negro servitude in the northern colonies. Englishmen there, like their countrymen in the southern colonies, inherited no legal basis for slavery; yet a slave status which fixed the Negro into a permanent caste position developed in New England, even though there the economic importance of the Negro was considerably less than in the South.[1] . . .

. . . It is also well known that the first Massachusetts legal code, the Body of Liberties of 1641, permitted enslavement of those who are "sold to us," which would apply to Negroes brought by the slave ships.

[1]This point is important because Oscar Handlin, *Race and Nationality in American Life* (New York, 1957), Chapter I, has attempted to explain the origins of slavery in terms of economic need. Obviously his argument cannot stand when tested in New England. There just were too few Negroes there in the seventeenth or eighteenth century to make an economic case for pushing the black man into a new status of slavery as Handlin contends. —Carl N. Degler

Nor was the use of Negroes as slaves unknown or undesirable to the Puritans. One correspondent of John Winthrop in 1645, for instance, talked of the desirability of war against the Indians, so that captives might be taken who could be exchanged "for Moores [Negroes], which will be more gayneful pilladge for us then [*sic*] wee conceive, for I doe not see how wee can thrive untill wee get into a stock of slaves sufficient to doe all our business, for our children's children will hardly see this great Continent filled with people. . . ." That enslavement of Negroes was well known in New England by the early 1650's is evident from the preamble of a Rhode Island statute of 1652. It was said that it "is a common course practised amongst Englishmen to buy Negers, to that end they may have them for service or slaves forever. . . ."

Though the number of Negroes in New England was exceedingly small, the colonies of that region followed the same path as the southern provinces in denying arms to the blacks in their midst. In 1652, Massachusetts had provided that Indians and Negroes should train in the militia the same as whites. But this ruling apparently caused friction, for in 1656 the earlier law was countermanded by the words "henceforth no Negroes or Indians, although servants of the English, shalbe armed or permitted to trayne." Connecticut in 1660 also excluded Indians and "Negar servants" from the militia . . . , although as late as 1680 it was officially reported to London that there were no more than thirty "slaves" in the colony.

Edward Randolph as commissioner of the Crown reported in 1676 that there were a few indentured servants in Massachusetts, "and not above two hundred slaves in the colony," by which he meant Negroes, for he said they "were brought from Guinea and Madagascar." Yet not until 1698 did the phrase "Negro slave" appear in the Massachusetts statutes. Practice was preceding law in New England just as it had in the South. In 1690, discrimination against the few Negroes in Connecticut reached the point where all Negroes were forbidden to be found outside the town bounds without "a ticket or a pass" from either master or the authorities, the restriction applying equally to free Negroes and slaves. Furthermore, it was provided that ferrymen would be fined if they permitted Negroes without passes to use their ferries. And though as early as 1680 official reports to London were distinguishing between slaves and servants, statute law barely defined the institution of slavery. In 1704, for example, the Governor gave it as his opinion that all children born of

"Negro bondwomen are themselves in like condition, i.e. born in servitude," but he admitted that no law had so provided. Legislation, he said, was "needless, because of the constant practice by which they are held as such. . . ." In 1717, Negroes were barred from holding land in Connecticut.

Thus, like the southern colonists, the New Englanders enacted into law, in the absence of any prior English law of slavery, their recognition of Negroes as different in race, religion, and culture. It should be especially noted that in many instances discriminations were made against all Negroes, whether slave or free—a fact which reinforces the argument that the discrimination . . . [led to] slavery and [was] not a consequence. Unquestionably, the coincidence of slavery with discrimination fastened still more firmly the stigma of inferiority upon the Negro, but slavery must be absolved of starting the cycle. It was the discriminatory attitude and behavior which conditioned the form slavery would take. . . . In this sense it might be proper to speak of slavery in the English colonies as the institutionalization of a folk prejudice. . . .

In time the correspondence between the black man and slavery would be so perfect that it would be difficult to realize that the Negro was not always and everywhere in a degraded status. Thus began in the seventeenth century the Negro's life in America. With it commenced a moral problem for all Americans which still besets us in the middle of the twentieth century.

PROBLEM 2

The Slave and the Plantation

Persistent and nagging questions face a student who studies the life of the Negro slave on Southern plantations before the Civil War. Was the slave a docile, contented, happy-go-lucky fellow whose leisure time was spent singing soulful melodies around the cabins, or was he surly and rebellious? Was the life of the slave marked by cruel beatings amid the worst possible working conditions, or was he treated with kindness and consideration in surroundings as good as those which poor peasants in Europe enjoyed? Did slaves on all plantations live in approximately the same way, or did working and living conditions differ from one slaveholder to another?

These questions are not easily answered. We are hampered in a search for the truth by the lack of completely reliable sources. Plantation records, the accounts of ex-slaves, and the observations of travelers from the North and from Europe provide the bulk of available information, and each of these sources is likely to reflect the prejudices and background of the writer.

For example, the life of an English gentleman may have been similar in many respects to the life of the owner of a large plantation.

In visiting the South, the Englishman may have overlooked the abuses of the system of slavery because he found living conditions for slaves as good as those for some of the free English laborers.

In reading each account, the student must always keep in mind the background of the person who wrote it. He must also keep in mind the different sorts of plantations on which the slaves lived.

On the eve of the Civil War about 4,000,000 slaves were held in the South by about 400,000 slaveholders. Ninety per cent of the slaveholders owned fewer than twenty Negroes; only ten per cent of the plantations fit the popular picture of a large estate manned by large groups of slaves. The differences in number meant great differences in how slaves lived. So did the type of crops raised and the various tasks to which slaves were assigned. Negroes living on a large sugar or rice plantation led quite different lives from laborers on small tobacco or cotton farms. On all plantations, field hands were treated differently from slaves who worked inside the mansion house.

All these distinctions—the size of the plantation, the type of crop, and the diverse tasks performed by slaves—make generalizations both difficult and risky. Of course, the character and personality of the individual slaveholder were equally important. One could be fatherly and kind; another could be cruel and vicious.

The first and second readings for Problem 2 were written by ex-slaves; the third by an English traveler; and the fourth by an English actress who became mistress of a Georgia rice plantation. As you read the selections, consider the following questions:

1   Do you detect any differences between the view of slavery held by Booker T. Washington and that of Frederick Douglass? Is there a difference in their views of Southern whites?

2   Do any of the writers reveal their attitudes toward slavery in their choice of words? For example, how does referring to a slave's house as "neat" rather than "filthy" reveal a bias?

3   How did each writer view the institution of slavery? Did any of them believe it was designed only to exploit the slaves? Did slavery provide food and shelter for those Negroes who were too old or too young to work?

4   Do the four authors agree about the way in which slaves were treated on plantations? Pay particular attention to the accounts of Lyell and Douglass.

5   Is it possible for all of these descriptions of plantation life to be accurate? Explain.

I

AN EX-SLAVE TELLS OF HIS CHILDHOOD

In his autobiography, Booker T. Washington, a prominent Negro educator and reformer of the early twentieth century, described his youth on a Virginia plantation before and during the Civil War. □ Booker T. Washington. *Up from Slavery.* New York: A. L. Burt Company, 1901, pp. 1–15 passim.

I was born a slave on a plantation in Franklin County, Virginia. I am not quite sure of the exact place or exact date of my birth, . . .

My life had its beginning in the midst of the most miserable, desolate, and discouraging surroundings. This was so, however, not because my owners were especially cruel, for they were not, as compared with many others. I was born in a typical log cabin, about fourteen by sixteen feet square. . . .

The cabin was not only our living-place, but was also used as the kitchen for the plantation. My mother was the plantation cook. The cabin was without glass windows; it had only openings in the side which let in the light, and also the cold, chilly air of winter. There was a door to the cabin—that is, something that was called a door—but the uncertain hinges by which it was hung, and the large cracks in it, to say nothing of the fact that it was too small, made the room a very uncomfortable one. . . . There was no wooden floor in our cabin, the naked earth being used as a floor. In the centre of the earthen floor there was a large, deep opening covered with boards, which was used as a place in which to store sweet potatoes during the winter.

The early years of my life, which were spent in the little cabin, were not very different from those of thousands of other slaves. My mother, of course, had little time in which to give attention to the training of her children during the day. She snatched a few moments for our care in the early morning before her work began, and at night after the day's work was done. One of my earliest recollections is that of my mother cooking a chicken late at night, and awakening her children for the purpose of feeding them. . . . I cannot remember having slept in a bed until after our family was declared free by the Emancipation Proclamation. Three children—John, my older brother, Amanda, my sister, and myself—had a pallet on the dirt floor, . . .

I had no schooling whatever while I was a slave, though I remember on several occasions I went as far as the schoolhouse door with one of my young mistresses to carry her books. The picture of several dozen boys and girls in a schoolroom engaged in study made a deep impression upon me, and I had the feeling that to get into the schoolhouse and study in this way would be about the same as getting into paradise. . . .

I cannot remember a single instance during my childhood or early boyhood when our entire family sat down to the table together, and God's blessing was asked, and the family ate a meal in a civilized manner. On the plantation in Virginia, and even later, meals were gotten by the children very much as dumb animals get theirs. It was a piece of bread here and a scrap of meat there. It was a cup of milk at one time and some potatoes at another. Sometimes a portion of our family would eat out of the skillet or pot, while some one would eat from a tin plate held on the knees, and often using nothing but the hands with which to hold the food. . . .

One may get the idea, from what I have said, that there was bitter feeling toward the white people on the part of my race, . . . In the case of the slaves on our place this was not true, and it was not true of any large portion of the slave population in the South where the Negro was treated with anything like decency. During the Civil War one of my young masters was killed, and two were severely wounded. I recall the feeling of sorrow which existed among the slaves when they heard of the death of "Mars' Billy." It was no sham sorrow, but real. Some of the slaves had nursed "Mars' Billy"; others had played with him when he was a child. "Mars' Billy" had begged for mercy in the case of others when the overseer or master was thrashing them. The sorrow in the slave quarter was only second to that in the "big house." . . . This tenderness and sympathy on the part of those held in bondage was a result of their kindly and generous nature. In order to defend and protect the women and children who were left on the plantations when the white males went to war, the slaves would have laid down their lives. The slave who was selected to sleep in the "big house" during the absence of the males was considered to have the place of honour. Anyone attempting to harm "young Mistress" or "old Mistress" during the night would have had to cross the dead body of the slave to do so. . . .

From some thing that I have said one may get the idea that some of the slaves did not want freedom. This is not true. I have never seen one who did not want to be free, or one who would return to slavery.

II

FREDERICK DOUGLASS TELLS HOW THE SLAVES LIVED

Frederick Douglass, Negro abolitionist, crusader for Negro equality, and government official, was born a slave on a Maryland plantation in 1817. When he was not yet seven years old, he was sent to Baltimore to live with a relative of his master and was taught to read and write by his new master's wife. Clashes between Douglass and the master resulted in his being sent to another plantation as a field hand. After an unsuccessful attempt to escape, he was sent again to Baltimore, where he learned the trade of a ship caulker, and in 1838, he finally made good his escape from slavery. Later, he became an active abolitionist speaker.

In 1845, when he published a *Narrative of the Life of Frederick Douglass*, he fled to Great Britain because information in the book could have led to his being captured as a fugitive slave. The following selection from his autobiography describes Douglass' boyhood on the Maryland plantation of Colonel Lloyd.   □ Frederick Douglass. *Life and Times of Frederick Douglass*. Boston: De Wolfe, Fiske and Company, 1892, pp. 62–64.

It was the boast of slaveholders that their slaves enjoyed more of the physical comforts of life than the peasantry of any country in the world. My experience contradicts this. The men and the women slaves on Col. Lloyd's farm received their monthly allowance of food, eight pounds of pickled pork, or its equivalent in fish. The pork was often tainted, and the fish were of the poorest quality. With their pork or fish, they had given them one bushel of Indian meal,   . . . of which quite fifteen per cent was more fit for pigs than for men. With this one pint of salt was given, and this was the entire monthly allowance of a full-grown slave, working constantly in the open field from morning till night every day in the month except Sunday.   . . . The yearly allowance of clothing was not more ample than the supply of food. It consisted of two tow-linen shirts, one pair of trowsers of the same coarse material for summer, and a woolen pair of trowsers and a woolen jacket for winter, with one pair of yarn stockings and a pair of shoes.   . . . Children under ten years old had neither shoes, stockings, jackets, nor trowsers. They had two coarse tow-linen shirts per year, and when these were worn out they went naked till the next allowance day—and this was the condition of the little girls as well as of the boys. As to beds, they had none. One coarse blanket was given them, and this only to the men and women. The children stuck themselves in holes and corners about the quarters, often in the corners of huge chimneys, with their feet in the ashes to keep them warm. The want of beds, however, was not considered a great privation by the field hands. Time to sleep was of far greater importance. For when the day's work was done most of these had their washing, mending, and cooking to do, and having few or no facilities for doing such things, very many of their needed sleeping hours were consumed in necessary preparations for the labors of the coming day. . . . Old and young, male and female, married and single, dropped down on the common clay floor, each covering up with his or her blanket, their only protection from cold or exposure. The night, however, was shortened at both ends. The slaves worked often as long as they could see, and were late in cooking and mending for the coming day, and at the first gray streak of the morning they were summoned to the field by the overseer's horn. They were whipped for over-sleeping more than for any other fault. . . . The overseer stood at the . . . door, armed with stick and whip, ready to deal heavy blows upon any who might be a little behind time. When the horn was blown there was a rush for the door, for the hindermost one was sure to get a blow from the overseer. Young mothers who worked in the field were allowed an hour about ten o'clock in the morning to go home to nurse their children.

III

AN ENGLISHMAN DESCRIBES HIS VISIT TO A PLANTATION

Sir Charles Lyell, a lecturer, writer, and renowned geologist of the early nineteenth century, visited the United States in 1841, 1845, 1852, and 1853. He had been educated at Oxford and was of an upper-class English family. After trying different vocations and traveling for a few years, he devoted the rest of his life to the scientific study of the structure of the earth. In the course of one of his trips to the United States, he toured the Hopeton plantation in Georgia and recorded his impressions. □ Sir Charles Lyell. *A Second Visit to the United States of North America.* London: J. Murray, 1849, pp. 262–266.

There are 500 negroes on the Hopeton estate, a great many of whom are children, and some old and superannuated. The latter class, who would be supported in a poor-house in England, enjoy here, to the end of their days, the society of their neighbors and kinsfolk, and live at large in separate houses assigned to them. The children have no regular work to do till they are ten or twelve years old. We see that some of them, at this season, are set to pick up dead leaves from the paths, others to attend the babies. . . .

The out-door laborers have separate houses provided for them; even the domestic servants, except a few who are nurses to the white children, live apart from the great house—an arrangement not always convenient for the masters, as there is no one to answer a bell after a certain hour. . . . The laborers begin work at six o'clock in the morning, have an hour's rest at nine for breakfast, and many have finished their assigned task by two o'clock, all of them by three o'clock. In summer they divide their work differently, going to bed in the middle of the day, then rising to finish their task, and afterward spending a great part of the night in chatting, merry-making, preaching, and psalm-singing. At Christmas they claim a week's holidays, when they hold a kind of Saturnalia, and the owners can get no work done. Although there is scarcely any drinking, the master rejoices when the season is well over without mischief. The negro houses are as neat as the greater part of the cottages in Scotland (no flattering compliment it must be confessed), are provided always with a back door, and a hall, as they call it, in which is a chest, a table, two or three chairs, and a few shelves for crockery. . . .

We visited the hospital at Hopeton, which consists of three separate wards, all perfectly clean and well-ventilated. One is for men, another for women, and a third for lying-in women. The latter are always allowed a month's rest after their confinement, an advantage rarely enjoyed by hard-working English peasants. . . .

The negro mothers are often so ignorant or indolent, that they can not be trusted to keep awake and administer medicine to their own children; so that the mistress [of the plantation] has often to sit up all night with a sick negro child. In submitting to this, they are actuated by mixed motives—a feeling of kindness, and a fear of losing the services of the slave; but these attentions greatly attach the negroes to their owners. In general, they refuse to take medicine from any other hands but those of their master or mistress. The laborers are allowed Indian meal, rice, and milk, and occasionally pork and soup. As their rations are more than they can eat, they either return part of it to the overseer, who makes them an allowance of money for it at the end of the week, or they keep it to feed their fowls, which they usually sell, as well as their eggs, for cash, to buy molasses, tobacco, and other luxuries. When disposed to exert themselves, they get through the day's task in five hours, and then amuse themselves in fishing, and sell the fish they take; or some of them employ their spare time in making canoes out of large cypress trees, leave being readily granted them to remove such timber, as it aids the land-owner to clear the swamps. They sell the canoes for about four dollars, for their own profit.

If the mistress pays a visit to Savannah, the nearest town, she is overwhelmed with commissions, so many of the slaves wishing to lay out their small gains in various indulgences, especially articles of dress, of which they are passionately fond. The stuff must be of the finest quality, and many instructions are given as to the precise color or fashionable shade. White muslin, with figured patterns, is the rage just now.

One day, when walking alone, I came upon a "gang" of negroes, who were digging a trench. They were superintended by a black "driver," who held a whip in his hand. Some of the laborers were using spades, others cutting away the roots and stumps of trees which they had encountered in the line of the ditch. Their mode of proceeding in their task was somewhat leisurely, and eight hours a day of this work are exacted, though they can accomplish the same in five hours, if they undertake it by the task. The digging of a given number of feet in length, breadth, and depth is, in this case, assigned to each ditcher, and a deduction made when they fall in with a stump or root. The names of gangs and drivers are odious, and the sight of the whip was painful to me as a mark of degradation, reminding me that the lower orders of slaves are kept to their work by mere bodily fear, and that their treatment must depend on the individual character of the owner or overseer. That the whip is rarely used, . . . is, I have no doubt, true on all well governed estates; . . . . It is a thong of leather, half an inch wide and a quarter of an inch thick. No ordinary driver is allowed to give more than six lashes for any offense, the head driver twelve, and the overseer twenty-four. When an estate is under superior management, the system is remarkably effective in preventing crime. . . .

Under the white overseer, the principal charge here is given to "Old Tom," the head driver, a man of superior intelligence . . . . He was the son of a prince of the Foulah tribe, and was taken prisoner, at the age of fourteen, near Timbuctoo. The accounts he gave of what he remembered of the plants and geography of Africa . . . confirm many of the narratives of modern travelers.

IV

AN ENGLISHWOMAN WRITES ABOUT HER HUSBAND'S SLAVES

Frances Anne ("Fanny") Kemble was a well-known English actress. She toured America in the early 1830's and married Pierce Butler, a member of an aristocratic Southern family. Before leaving for the South, Fanny promised to write her friend Elizabeth Sedgwick, who was a passionate opponent of slavery, of her experiences on Butler's cotton and rice plantations. In a series of letters Fanny described her reactions to slavery, and later she released her letters for book publication, hoping that her description of Southern conditions would sway Great Britain to support the Union instead of the Confederacy. □ Frances Anne Kemble. *Journal of a Residence on a Georgian Plantation.* New York: Harper and Brothers, 1863, pp. 30–33, 43, 189–191 passim.

I walked down the settlement toward the Infirmary or hospital, calling in at one or two of the houses along the row. These cabins consist of one room, about twelve feet by fifteen, with a couple of closets smaller and closer than the state-rooms of a ship, divided off from the main room and each other by rough wooden partitions, in which the inhabitants sleep. They have almost all of them a rude bedstead, with the gray moss of the forests for mattress, and filthy, pestilential-looking blankets for covering. Two families (sometimes eight and ten in number) reside in one of these huts, which are mere wooden frames pinned, as it were, to the earth by a brick chimney outside, whose enormous aperture within pours down a flood of air, but little counteracted by the miserable spark of fire, . . . Firewood and shavings lay littered about the floors, while the half-naked children were cowering round two or three smouldering cinders. . . . In the midst of the floor, or squatting round the cold hearth, would be four or five little children from four to ten years old, the latter all with babies in their arms, the care of the infants being taken from the mothers . . . .

The Infirmary is a large two-story building, terminating the broad orange-planted space between the two rows of houses which form the first settlement; it is built of whitewashed wood, and contains four large-sized rooms. . . . In the enormous chimney glimmered the powerless embers of a few sticks of wood, round which, however, as many of the sick women as could approach were cowering, some on wooden settles, most of them on the ground, excluding those who were too ill to rise; and these last poor wretches lay prostrate on the floor, without bed, mattress, or pillow, buried in tattered and filthy blankets, which, huddled round them as they lay strewed about, left hardly space to move upon the floor. And here, in their hour of sickness and suffering, lay those whose health and strength are spent in unrequited labor for us—those who, perhaps even yesterday, were being urged on to their unpaid task—those whose husbands, fathers, brothers, and sons were even at that hour sweating over the earth, whose produce was to buy for us all the luxuries which health can revel in, all the comforts which can alleviate sickness. . . . Here lay women . . . burning with fever, others chilled with cold and aching with rheumatism, upon the hard cold ground, the draughts and dampness of the atmosphere increasing their sufferings, and dirt, noise, and stench, . . .

At the upper end of the row of houses, and nearest to our overseer's residence, is the hut of the head driver. . . . Each driver is allowed to inflict a dozen lashes upon any refractory slave in the field, and at the time of the offense; . . . and if it is found ineffectual, their remedy lies in reporting the unmanageable individual either to the head driver or the overseer, the former of whom has power to inflict three dozen lashes at his own discretion . . . ; and as for the master himself, where is his limit? He may, if he likes, flog a slave to death, for the laws which pretend that he may not are a mere pretense, inasmuch as the testimony of a black is never taken against a white; and upon this plantation of ours, and a thousand more, the overseer is the *only* white man, so whence should come the testimony to any crime of his? With regard to the oft-repeated statement that it is not the owner's interest to destroy his human property, it answers nothing; . . . Nothing is commoner than for a man under the transient influence of anger to disregard his worldly advantage; and the black slave, whose preservation is indeed supposed to be his owner's interest, may be, will be, and is occasionally sacrificed to the blind impulse of passion. . . .

Before closing this letter, I have a mind to transcribe to you the entries for to-day recorded in a sort of daybook . . . the number of people who visit me, their petitions and ailments, and also such special particulars concerning them as seem to me worth recording. . . . Judge from the details I now send you; and never forget, while reading them, that the people on this plantation are well off, and consider themselves well off, in comparison with the slaves on some of the neighboring estates.

Fanny has had six children; all dead but one. She came to beg to have her work in the field lightened.

Nanny has had three children; two of them are dead. She came to implore that the rule of sending them into the field three weeks after their confinement might be altered.

Leah, Caesar's wife, has had six children; three are dead.

Sophy, Lewis's wife, came to beg for some old linen. She is suffering fearfully; has had ten children; five of them are dead. The principal favor she asked was a piece of meat, which I gave her.

Sally, Scipio's wife, has had two miscarriages and three children born, one of whom is dead. She came complaining of incessant pain and weakness in her back. This woman was a mulatto daughter of a slave called Sophy, by a white man of the name of Walker, who visited the plantation.

Charlotte, Renty's wife, had had two miscarriages, and was with child again. She was almost crippled with rheumatism, and showed me a pair of poor swollen knees that made my heart ache. I have promised her a pair of flannel trowsers, which I must forthwith set about making.

Sarah, Stephen's wife — this woman's case and history were alike deplorable. She had had four miscarriages, had brought seven children into the world, five of whom were dead, and was again with child. She complained of dreadful pains in the back, and an internal tumor which swells with the exertion of working in the fields; probably, I think, she is ruptured. She told me she had once been mad and had ran into the woods, where she contrived to elude discovery for some time, but was at last tracked and brought back, when she was tied up by the arms, and heavy logs fastened to her feet, and was severely flogged.   .   .   .

Sukey, Bush's wife, only came to pay her respects. She had had four miscarriages, had brought eleven children into the world, five of whom are dead.

Molly, Quambo's wife, also only came to see me. Hers was the best account I have yet received; she had had nine children, and six of them were still alive.

This is only the entry for to-day, in my diary, of the people's complaints and visits. Can you conceive a more wretched picture than that which it exhibits of the conditions under which these women live?

PROBLEM 3

Free Negroes
Before the Civil War

Even before the Civil War, many American Negroes had won their freedom. In 1790, about 59,000 free Negroes lived in the North and South. By 1860, the number had increased to about 488,000.

From the late eighteenth century until the Civil War, a number of slaveholders had released Negroes in various ways. John Randolph, a Virginia planter, freed 518 slaves in his will. With $30,000 that Randolph left them, 395 of these new freedmen settled in southern Ohio. In some cases, planters permitted slaves to buy their freedom with money earned by various services performed for persons other than their owners. In the 1830's a Samuel Lewis of Cincinnati paid $500 for himself. David Young of the same city bought his wife and six children for $1265.

In addition, the number of free Negroes grew, especially in the North, by the thousands of runaway slaves who escaped by means of the "Underground Railroad." Quakers, free Negroes, and abolitionists helped the runaways to reach free soil by acting as "conductors" at the various "depots" along Underground Railroad "routes."

Finally, natural increase raised the total number of free Negroes.

With family life among freedmen becoming more stable, children added to the number, and children born of free Negro mothers were generally considered free.

Free Negroes in the North and South had to surmount innumerable barriers, including the adjustment to meeting the responsibilities of freedom. Many did adjust. In 1837 free Negroes of New York City owned taxable real estate valued at $1,400,000 and had $600,000 on deposit in savings banks. In many communities, Negroes who had learned trades or professions earned their living as craftsmen or businessmen. Included among them were barbers, carpenters, bricklayers, dentists, architects, and lawyers. A few free Negroes even became slaveholders.

However, most Negroes were still barred from white society. Hostility, discrimination, and abuse characterized race relations in both North and South. Although many Northerners opposed the extension of slavery, they did not guarantee equality to the individual free Negro or provide opportunities for his progress. The combined obstacles of white prejudice, poverty, illiteracy, and lack of educational and employment opportunities served to force most Northern Negroes into urban slums. Here, the social conditions under which they lived tended to reinforce white prejudices.

The readings selected for Problem 3 describe the conditions of the freedmen in the era before the Civil War. Those in the first section present views of some Ohio legislators on free Negroes; those in the second describe some conditions confronting free Negroes in the North; the last section offers the opinions of a few free Negroes. In reading these selections, consider the following questions:

1 What are the arguments put forth in the first reading to exclude free Negroes from the state of Ohio? Compare these arguments to those used by Southern segregationists today.

2 Was life difficult for a free Negro in the North? Cite specific evidence.

3 In the second part of the third reading, Frederick Douglass writes about Thomas L. Jennings. Contrast his account of the life of this Negro with the opinions expressed about Negroes in general in Reading I of this Problem.

4 Many Southern planters pointed out that free Negroes in the North suffered discrimination, abuse, and lack of opportunity and were consequently not so well off as their racial brothers in slavery. Do you agree? Consider Problem 2, "The Slave and the Plantation."

I

SOME WHITE OPINIONS OF FREE NEGROES

By 1832 so many Negroes had won their freedom that the legislatures of Virginia and other slave states were taking measures for strict policing of the freedmen. "This must soon render their situation intolerable, and their emigration from that State [Virginia] almost a matter of necessity," said a member of the Committee on the Colored Population of Ohio. To escape the policing laws, thousands of free Negroes, as well as fugitive slaves, were migrating northward, particularly to Ohio. After investigating the situation, the committee reported to the Ohio legislature. ☐ *The Ohio State Journal, and Columbus Gazette.* Columbus, Ohio: February 1, 1832, p. 1.

Even now, when this people constitute less than one hundredth part of our population, the evils arising from their residence amongst us are seriously felt, and especially where they are congregated in considerable numbers in the larger towns.

By the exclusion of a large amount of labor of white men, who will not degrade themselves . . . [by competing] with blacks:

By the demoralization of those white citizens who do, by association with, . . . blacks, lose that standing and consideration in society, which is one of the strongest safeguards . . . :

By the habits of . . . petty pilfering, which are, and must of necessity be prevalent, among a people isolated in society, and deprived of the highest motives to honest industry . . . :

And lastly, by the injurious effects upon our youth. . . .

While we admit, in its fullest extent, the right of our sister States to adopt all such measures as they may deem proper for their own security, we do most earnestly protest against the intrusion amongst us of a rejected and dangerous population. . . .

Eighteen years later, at the Ohio Constitutional Convention, delegates were hearing arguments on whether or not Negroes should be allowed to vote. ☐ Report of the Debates and Proceedings of the Convention for the Revision of the Constitution of the State of Ohio 1850–51, pp. 57–58.

Mr. Brown [of Athens County] said he did not wish it to be understood here or elsewhere, that he would vote for extending the right of suffrage to the African race. They were considered a degraded people among us, for what reason it was not his purpose to inquire, the opinion obtained however, and they could not, by force of public authority, bring them on an equality with the white race. Until there was an entire social revolution in the intercourse between the two races—until the time came when the black man could go to your house as a suitor for your daughter, and ask and obtain her in marriage, and until you could welcome the issue of that marriage, and receive with pride your little grandson "William Cuffy," or some such name, that would follow—and when a man could introduce them to his friends, and they would be received into the society of the white race—until then the two races were separate and distinct. When this revolution had taken place in the intercourse between the negro and us, then would be the proper time to give them the right of suffrage. He considered that extending the right of suffrage to our colored population would be productive of serious inconveniences; in his opinion it would have a tendency to degrade labor.

II

EXPERIENCES OF FREE NEGROES IN THE NORTH

In 1832 the town of Canterbury, Connecticut, protested violently when a boarding school for young Negro girls was proposed. William Jay, an abolitionist, told of the incident. ☐ William Jay. An Inquiry into the Character and Tendency of the American Colonization and American Anti-Slavery Societies. New York: Leavitt and Lord, 1835, pp. 30–31.

Miss Crandall, a member in the Baptist church, and . . . a lady of irreproachable character, had for some time been at the head of a female boarding school, in the town of Canterbury, Connecticut, when in the autumn of 1832, a pious colored female applied to her for admission into her school, stating that she wanted "to get a little more learning—enough if possible to teach colored children." After some hesitation, Miss Crandall consented to admit her, but was soon informed that this intruder must be dismissed, or that the school would be greatly injured. This threat turned her attention to the cruel prejudices and disadvantages under which the blacks are suffering, and she resolved to open a school exclusively for colored girls. . . . This notice excited prodigious commotion in the town of Canterbury. That black girls should presume to learn reading, and writing, and music, and geography, was past all bearing. Committee after committee waited on Miss Crandall, to remonstrate against the intended school, but to no purpose. More efficient means were found necessary to avert the impending calamity, and a legal town meeting was summoned to consider the awful crisis. At this meeting resolutions were passed, expressing the strongest disapproval of the proposed school, and the preamble declared that "the obvious tendency of this school would be to collect within the town of Canterbury, large numbers of persons from other States, whose characters and habits might be various and unknown to us, thereby rendering insecure the *persons, property, and reputations* of our citizens." Had this extreme nervous apprehension of danger, been excited in the good people of Canterbury, by the introduction of some hundreds of Irish laborers into their village to construct a rail road or canal, we should still have thought their temperament very peculiar; but when we find them thus affecting to tremble not merely for their property, but for their *persons* and *reputations*, at the approach of fifteen or twenty "young ladies and little misses of color," we confess we are astonished that the collected wisdom of these people was not able to frame an argument against the school, less disgraceful to themselves.

In a letter dated October 26, 1838, Thomas Van Renselaer, a Negro abolitionist, reported an experience he had on a steamboat to his friend, Joshua Leavitt of Boston.   ☐ *The Liberator.* Boston: November 30, 1838, p. 189.

REV. JOSHUA LEAVITT—Dear Brother.—I stepped on board the Steamboat J. W. Richmond, in your city, yesterday afternoon, for Providence. I had previously understood that *this* being an opposition [or integrated] boat, people were treated irrespective of complexion; so, full of hope of a pleasant entertainment, I went to the office and paid $3.50 (fifty cents more than the regular fare,) for my passage and a berth, No. 15, which was assigned me in the after cabin, and obtained my ticket. I walked about until dark, when, feeling chilly, I repaired to the cabin in which my berth was. I had not been there long, before a man came up to me in a very abrupt manner, and said, 'Whose servant are you?' I at first gave no answer; he repeated, and I replied, I am my own, Sir. 'Well,' said he, 'you must go on deck.' I asked, why so? 'Because you ought to know your place.' I said, this is my place. Said he, 'Go on deck, I tell you.' Said I, I cannot go on deck. Said he with an oath, and running upon deck, 'I'll make you.' He returned in a moment with the captain, who came trembling, and said, 'I want you to go on deck immediately.' I asked the reason. 'Not a word from you, sir.' I asked, what offence have I committed? 'Not a word, sir,' said he, and laid hold of me with violence, and ordered two men to remove me. But when I saw him in such a rage, and fearing that he might do *himself* harm, I retired, and walked the deck till late in the night, when I had another talk with the captain. I then told him he had not treated me well, and that an explanation was due from him; but he refused to allow me to go below, or to give me a berth. I then told him I should publish the treatment I had received. He again flew in a passion, and I said no more to him. Between 11 and 12 o'clock, one of the waiters invited me to occupy a bed which he had prepared. I accepted it, and was rendered comfortable; and feel very grateful to three of the waiters for their sympathy in these trying moments, as well as to some of the passengers. One gentleman in particular, the Rev. Mr. Scudder, (Methodist) gave me great consolation by identifying himself with me at the time.

Now, dear brother, I have made this communication of facts for the information of the friends of human rights, who, I believe, have patronized *this boat* from principle, that they may act understandingly hereafter. Yours in affliction,   THOS. VAN RENSELAER.

William Wells Brown, an abolitionist, described the kidnapping of a free Negro in a letter dated September 27, 1844, to Sydney H. Gay, editor of the *National Anti-Slavery Standard*.   ☐ *National Anti-Slavery Standard*. New York: November 7, 1844, p. 90.

DEAR FRIEND GAY:—I left Cadiz this morning . . . on my way for Mount Pleasant. Passing through Georgetown at about five o'clock, I found the citizens standing upon the corners of the streets, talking as though something had occurred during the night. Upon inquiry, I learned that about ten o'clock at night, five or six men went to the house of a colored man by the name of John Wilkinson, broke open the door, knocked down the man and his wife, and beat them severely, and seized their boy, aged fourteen years, and carried him off into Slavery. After the father of the boy had recovered himself, he raised the alarm, and with the aid of some of the neighbors, put out in pursuit of the kidnappers, and followed them to the river; but they were too late. The villains crossed the river, and passed into Virginia. I visited the afflicted family this morning. When I entered the house, I found the mother seated with her face buried in her hands, weeping for the loss of her child. The mother was much bruised, and the floor was covered in several places with blood. I had been in the house but a short time, when the father returned from the chase of the kidnappers. When he entered the house, and told the wife that their child was lost forever, the mother wrung her hands and screamed out, "Oh, my boy! I want to see my child!" and raved as though she was a maniac. I was compelled to turn aside and weep for the first time since I came into the State. I would that every Northern apologist for Slavery, could have been present to have beheld that scene. I hope to God that it may never be my lot to behold another such. One of the villains was recognized, but it was by a colored man, and the colored people have not the right of their oath in this State. This villain will go unwhipped of Justice. What have the North to do with Slavery? Ever yours, for the slave.   WM. W. BROWN.

Living conditions for free Negroes in the North are described by a present-day historian. ☐ Leon F. Litwack. *North of Slavery*. Chicago: University of Chicago Press, 1961, pp. 168–170.

Economic exploitation and segregation produced the Negro ghetto. In Boston, Negroes congregated on "Nigger Hill" and along the wharves in "New Guinea"; in Cincinnati, they crowded into wooden shacks and shanties in "Little Africa"; in New York, they concentrated in a few wards and mixed with poor whites in the notorious "Five Points," described by one visitor as "but a step into Hades" and "the worst hell of America"; and in Philadelphia, they settled in gloomy cellars and squalid houses located along narrow courts and alleys. Although some observers also pointed to the remarkable number of fine houses owned by Negroes in attractive neighborhoods, few could turn their eyes from the squalor of the Negro slums or deny their existence. To southern visitors in the North, such conditions demonstrated the folly of emancipation. "Thar they was," one southerner [William T. Thompson] wrote [in *Major Jones's Sketches of Travel*], "covered with rags and dirt, livin in houses and cellars, without hardly any furniture; and sum of 'em without dores or winders. . . . This, thinks I, is nigger freedom; this is the condition to which the philanthropists of the North wants to bring the happy black people of the South!"

Such surroundings obviously had their impact on the general health of the Negro residents. In New York City, tuberculosis proved fatal to twice as many blacks as whites, a reflection of adverse living conditions. Philadelphia's coroner attributed the high mortality rate in Negro districts to intemperance, exposure, and malnutrition. After conducting an inspection in 1848, he reported that many Negroes had been "found dead in cold and exposed rooms and garrets, board shanties five and six feet high, and as many feet square, erected and rented for lodging purposes, mostly without any comforts, save the bare floor, with the cold penetrating between the boards, and through the holes and crevices on all sides." Some bodies had been recovered "in cold, wet, and damp cellars," while still others had been found lying in back yards and alleys. . . .

The vigorous exclusion of Negroes from white residential neighborhoods made escape from the ghetto virtually impossible. The fear of depreciated property values overrode virtually every other consideration. As early as 1793, the attempt to locate "a Negro hut" in Salem, Massachusetts, prompted a white minister to protest that such buildings depreciated property, drove out decent residents, and generally injured the welfare of the neighborhood. Some years later, New Haven petitioners complained that the movement of Negroes into previously white neighborhoods deteriorated real estate values from 20 to 50 per cent; an Indianan asserted that the proposed establishment of a Negro tract would reduce the value of nearby white-owned lots by at least 50 per cent. Obviously, then, the Negro had to be contained in his own area. Thus when a Boston Negro schoolmistress considered moving to a better neighborhood, the inhabitants of the block where she proposed to settle resolved either to eject her or to destroy the house. By 1847, the residents of South Boston could boast that "not a single colored family" lived among them — only immigrants "of the better class who will not live in cellars."

Although whites frequently deprecated the Negro slums, some profited from them. In Cincinnati's Little Africa, for example, whites owned most of the wooden shacks and shanties and protested the attempt of municipal authorities to bar further construction of wooden buildings in the center of town. "Heaven preserve the shanties," a Cincinnati editor [Richard C. Wade, in "The Negro in Cincinnati, 1800–1830"] sarcastically remarked, "and supply the proprietors with tenants from whom the rent can be screwed, without respect to color or character." While white critics continued to deplore Negro housing conditions, white landlords made few, if any, improvements. Both conveniently concluded that Negroes naturally lived that way.

III

SOME NEGRO OPINIONS OF FREE NEGROES

In an address to the people of California, members of the First State Convention of the Colored Citizens of the State of California appealed for equality and reminded the people of the contributions that Negroes had made to the state. □ J. H. Townsend, for the State Executive Committee. Proceedings of the First State Convention of the Colored Citizens of the State of California. Democratic State Journal Print. Sacramento: 1855, pp. 26–27.

The colored citizens of this Commonwealth, would [respectfully] represent before you, their state and condition; and they respectfully ask a candid and careful investigation of facts in relation to their true character.

Our population numbers about 6,000 persons, who own capital to the amount of near $3,000,000. This has been accumulated by our own industry, since we migrated to the shores of the Pacific.

Most of us were born upon your soil; reared up under the influence of your institutions; become familiar with your manners and customs; acquired most of your habits, and adopted your policies. We yield allegiance to no other country save this. With all her faults we love her still.

Our forefathers were among the first who took up arms and fought side by side with yours; poured out their blood freely in the struggle for American independence. They fought, as they had every reason to suppose, the good fight of liberty, until it finally triumphed.

In the war of 1812, in which you achieved independence and glory upon the seas, the colored men, were also among the foremost to engage in the conflict, rendering efficient service in behalf of their common country. Through a long series of years have we been always ready to lay down our lives for the common weal, in defense of the national honor. On the other hand, instead of treating us as good and loyal citizens, you have treated us as aliens; sought to degrade us in all walks of life; condemned us in Church and State as an ignorant and debased class, unworthy of the sympathy and regard of men; without examining into our true character, you have allowed yourselves to become bitterly prejudiced against us. . . .

We again call upon you to regard our condition in the State of California. We point with pride to the general character we maintain in your midst, for integrity, industry, and thrift. You have been wont to multiply our vices, and never to see our virtues. You call upon us to pay enormous taxes to support Government, at the same time you deny us the protection you extend to others; the security for life and property. You require us to be good citizens, while seeking to degrade us. You ask why we are not more intelligent? You receive our money to educate your children, and then refuse to admit our children into the common schools. You have enacted a law, excluding our testimony in the Courts of justice of this State, in cases of proceedings wherein white persons are parties; thus openly encouraging and countenancing the vicious and dishonest to take advantage of us; a law, which, while it does not advantage you, is a great wrong to us. At the same time, you freely admit the evidence of men in your midst, who are ignorant of the first principles of your Government—who know not the alphabet. Many colored men, who have been educated in your first colleges, are not allowed to testify! and wherefore? our Divine Father has created us with a darker complexion.

People of California! we entreat you to repeal that unjust law.

Frederick Douglass had been born a Negro slave. After his escape to freedom, he became an abolitionist. In his journal, *Frederick Douglass's Paper*, he praised a Negro tailor, Thomas L. Jennings, who died February 11, 1859. □ *The Anglo-African Magazine.* New York: April 1859, pp. 126–127.

Mr. Jennings was a native of New York, and in his early youth was one of the bold men of color who, in this then slave State, paraded the streets of the metropolis with a banner inscribed with the figure of a black man, and the words 'AM I NOT A MAN AND A BROTHER?' He was one of the colored volunteers who aided in digging trenches on Long Island in the war of 1812. He took a leading part in the celebration of the abolition of slavery in New York in 1827. . . . When in 1830 Wm. Lloyd Garrison came on from Baltimore, Mr. Jennings was among the colored men of New York, . . . who gave him a cordial welcome and God-speed, and subscribed largely to establish the *Liberator*. . . .

He was an actor in the great meeting in Chatham Street Chapel. He was a leading member of the first, second and third of the National Conventions of colored men of the United States, held in New York and Philadelphia in 1831–4. He was one of the originators of the Legal Rights' Association in New York city, and President thereof at the time of his death. His suit against the Third Avenue Railroad Company for ejecting his daughter from one of its cars on Sabbath day, led to the abolition of caste in cars in four out of the five city railroads. He was one of the founders, and during many years a trustee of the Abyssinian Baptist Church.

In his boyhood, Mr. Jennings served an apprenticeship with one of the most celebrated of the New York tailors. Soon after reaching manhood, he entered business on his own account, and invented a method of renovating garments, for which he obtained letters patent from the United States. Although it was well known that he was a black man of 'African descent,' these letters recognize him as a 'citizen of the United States.' This document, in an antique gilded frame, hangs above the bed in which Mr. Jennings breathed his last, and is signed by the historic names of John Quincy Adams and William Wirt, and bears the broad seal of the United States of America.

For many years Mr. Jennings conducted a successful business as Clothier, in Nassau and Chatham streets.

Mr. Jennings had a large family, whom he educated carefully and successfully, both in intellectual and moral training. He taught all his children some useful trade, and accustomed them betimes to rely on themselves for their support. His son William died twenty years ago, a successful business man in Boston; Thomas was until lately, one of the most skilful dentists in New Orleans; his daughter, Matilda is one of the best dress makers in New York city, and Elizabeth the most learned of our female teachers in the city of New York, having obtained mainly through her own labor, the honor of a diploma from the Board of Education of said city.

This is a noble picture of a noble man. Born in a slave State, and of a race held in slavery, living in the midst of all the crushing influences which human prejudice and caste could heap upon him, he yet fulfilled all the purposes of an upright man, a useful citizen, and a devoted Christian; . . . He upheld society by an active, earnest and blameless life, and by contributing thereto children carefully trained to conduce to the general good. Not gifted with extraordinary talents or endowments, he made full use of such as it had pleased God to give him.

Mr. Jennings was one of that large class of earnest, upright colored men who dwell in our large cities. He was not an exception, but a representative of this class, whose noble sacrifices . . . are too little known to the public. — *Fred. Douglass' Paper.*

PROBLEM 4

The Negro and the Civil War

Over 600,000 Americans died in the Civil War, the bloodiest in American history. Both whites and Negroes suffered casualties. Of the almost 200,000 Negro troops who took part in over 190 battles, approximately 68,000 of them were killed or wounded.

Participation of Negroes as soldiers was, however, a privilege denied to them until the war was two years old. The delay was due chiefly to Northern fears and doubts. Would the Negro fight well? How would Northern whites react to fighting with Negroes? How would Southerners feel about arming Negroes? Apparently whites had forgotten that Negroes fought with distinction in the Revolutionary War and in the War of 1812.

Though anxieties existed, Northern defeats and mounting casualty rates brought a drop in fighting morale and forced the issue. A few months after the Emancipation Proclamation, Negroes were officially permitted to enlist as combat soldiers. Frederick Douglass' sons were among the first to volunteer for Massachusetts' two colored regiments.

Even with Negroes flocking to the colors, the doubts about the value of Negroes as soldiers persisted, and Negro troops at first experienced discriminatory treatment. White privates earned thirteen dollars a month; Negro privates received seven. Negro soldiers built roads, cooked, and cleaned, but did little fighting until tremendous battlefield losses forced the use of Negro troops on the front lines. Favorable reports about the Negro's ability to fight brought respect and eventual removal of inequalities. As a result, Negro troops took part in major and minor military actions for the duration of the war.

The selections for Problem 4 tell about the use of Negro troops. In reading, keep the following questions in mind:

1   Why were Negro troops used?

2   Of what significance was it for the nation that Negroes were armed and permitted to fight for freedom?

3   Would Colonel Griffin's letter have been written if General Wild's troops had not been Negro? Why did Southerners dislike the use of Negroes as soldiers by the Union army?

4   Do the accounts of the battle at Fort Pillow reveal the brutality of war or anti-Negro feelings on the part of the Confederates?

I

THE UNION ARMY DECIDES TO USE NEGRO SOLDIERS

Reasons for using or not using Negro troops in the federal armies were many, but necessity eventually overrode all other considerations. A Civil War historian views the reaction to the decision to recruit Negroes and tells of the effect of the decision on Negroes in America. ☐ From *This Hallowed Ground*, by Bruce Catton, pp. 222–227. Copyright © 1955, 1956 by Bruce Catton. Reprinted by permission of Doubleday & Company, Inc.

This decision to use the Negro as a soldier did not necessarily grow out of any broad humanitarian resolve; it seems to have come largely out of the dawning realization that, since the Confederates were going to kill a great many more Union soldiers before the war was over, a good many white men would escape death if a considerable percentage of those soldiers were colored.

[General Henry W.] Halleck put the thing quite bluntly in a message to Grant in March [1863]. It was good policy, he said, to withdraw as many slaves from the South as possible; equally good policy, having withdrawn them, to use them to help win the war. They could certainly be used as teamsters and as laborers, and some people believed they could be used as combat soldiers. Grant must try, and if he found—as he undoubtedly would—that many of the people in his army objected to it, he must ride their objections down and see that this new policy was carried out.

"There can be no peace," wrote Halleck, "but that which is forced by the sword. We must conquer the Rebels or be conquered by them. . . . This is the phase which the rebellion has now assumed. We must take things as they are."

This new phase of the rebellion was a good deal broader than Halleck dreamed. To accept the Negro as a soldier was to state, in a back-handed but decisive way, that the base of membership in the American community had been immeasurably widened. . . . For the war had become a breaking up of the foundations of the great deep, and to "take things as they are" meant to change things to their fundamentals. . . .

Removing the prejudice would not be easy. Soldiers who disliked slavery very often looked upon the slaves themselves as subhuman creatures who belonged neither in the army nor in America itself. An Illinois veteran wrote from Tennessee that he and many others would be emancipationists "if the brutes could be shipped out of the country," but that did not seem to be possible. Slavery, he admitted, was "an awful sin," but if Negroes had to remain in America they ought to remain as slaves; the only suggestion he could make was that they be transferred from Confederate masters to masters thoroughly loyal to the Union.

An Ohio soldier reported that there was intense opposition in his division to the recruiting of Negro troops, . . . with officers and enlisted men vowing that they would throw down their arms and go home if Negroes became soldiers.

This . . . opposition was quickly tamped down . . . . .

The division in which the Ohio soldier had reported so much discontent was . . . addressed by [General Lorenzo] Thomas. Men who left the army because of the recruiting of Negroes, he warned, would be considered guilty of treason and would be shot, and there would be courts-martial for all who interfered with the program. The boys talked it over around campfires afterward and concluded finally that "a Negro could stop a bullet just as well as a white man," and that "for everyone so sacrificed there would be just that many more white soldiers to return north to their families and friends." . . .

Negroes could stop bullets . . . ; they could also open the avenue for promotion to white soldiers. The new colored regiments would need officers. The officers, except in the rarest cases, would not be colored; they would be white men, combat veterans, selected from the ranks of the line regiments, given a quick course . . . in an officer-training school, and then commissioned as lieutenants, captains, or even better. The veterans perked up their ears at this news. Some of those who had been most bitter about the new program became reconciled to it when they considered that they themselves, as a result of it, might wear shoulder straps. There was no lack of candidates for the training schools. . . . In one way or another, colored regiments were called into being, officered, and put to work.

There was a great deal of self-interest in the decision to turn Negroes into soldiers, but there was also the pressure of sheer necessity. The contraband slave was becoming uncommonly numerous; simply by his insistence on fleeing from bondage and by his mute faith that the nearest Federal army would be his sure protector — he was compelling the authorities to do something with him, and very often the easiest thing to do was to put him into uniform. . . .

Almost to a man the male contrabands were eager to enlist when the chance was offered. Yet disillusionment usually came soon afterward. It was hard for generals to think of them as combat troops; for the most part the Negro was looked upon as a sort of servant to the white soldiers, he got much more than his full share of fatigue duty, and in some camps he was excused from drill altogether so that he might dig ditches, raise fortifications, and perform other pick-and-shovel work. When they were kept at this non-military work, it was noted, most colored soldiers became restive, sullen, sometimes insubordinate.

In the main, though, the newly enlisted Negro was intensely proud of his status as soldier. His pride could be surprising at times, because it seemed to go deeper than mere pride in a musket and a uniform and became pride in a new status as a human being. . . .

. . . And the eloquent former slave Frederick Douglass, who had worked and hoped long to see his people brought to freedom, saw even more in it than that:

"Once let the black man get upon his person the brass letters, U.S.; let him get an eagle on his button, and a musket on his shoulder and bullets in his pocket, and there is no power on earth which can deny that he has earned the right to citizenship in the United States."

II

A UNION GENERAL PRAISES NEGRO TROOPS

On May 30, 1863, after the siege of Vicksburg had begun, General Nathaniel P. Banks wrote to Major-General Henry W. Halleck, general-in-chief of the United States army. After reporting on the battles in which his men had engaged the enemy, General Banks went on to tell how his troops had behaved under fire. ☐ Henry Carey Baird, Compiler. *Washington and Jackson on Negro Soldiers.* Philadelphia: 1863.

HEADQUARTERS ARMY OF THE GULF,
BEFORE PORT HUDSON, May 30, 1863.

Major-General H. W. Halleck, General-in-Chief, Washington.

GENERAL: — Leaving Sommesport on the Atchafalaya, where my command was at the date of my last dispatch, I landed at Bayou Sara at 2 o'clock on the morning of the 21st. . . .

In the assault of the 27th, the behavior of the officers and men was most gallant, and left nothing to be desired. Our limited acquaintance of the ground and the character of the works, which were almost hidden from our observation until the moment of approach, alone prevented the capture of the post.

On the extreme right of our line I posted the first and third regiments of negro troops. The First regiment of Louisiana Engineers, composed exclusively of colored men, excepting the officers, was also engaged in the operations of the day. The position occupied by these troops was one of importance, and called for the utmost steadiness and bravery in those to whom it was confided.

It gives me pleasure to report that they answered every expectation. Their conduct was heroic. No troops could be more determined or more daring. They made, during the day, three charges upon the batteries of the enemy, suffering very heavy losses, and holding their position at nightfall with the other troops on the right of our line. The highest commendation is bestowed upon them by all the officers in command on the right. Whatever doubt may have existed before as to the efficiency of organizations of this character, the history of this day proves conclusively to those who were in a condition to observe the conduct of these regiments, that the Government will find in this class of troops effective supporters and defenders.

The severe test to which they were subjected, and the determined manner in which they encountered the enemy, leave upon my mind no doubt of their ultimate success. They require only good officers, commands of limited numbers, and careful discipline, to make them excellent soldiers.

Our losses from the 23d to this date in killed, wounded, and missing, are nearly 1000, including, I deeply regret to say, some of the ablest officers of the corps. I am unable yet to report them in detail.

I have the honor to be, with much respect,

Your Obedient servant,

N. P. BANKS, *Major-General Commanding.*

III

A CONFEDERATE COLONEL CONDEMNS NEGRO SOLDIERS

A raid by Negro troops of the Union army in North Carolina drove Confederate guerrillas from one part of that state. Following the raid, Colonel Joel R. Griffin of the Confederate forces wrote to the Union commander of the Negro troops, General Edward A. Wild. ☐ Frank Moore, Editor. *Rebellion Record,* 1864–5. New York: D. Van Nostrand, 1865, pp. 304–305.

HEADQUARTERS FORCES ON BLACKWATER,
FRANKLIN, VA., January, 1864.
General Wild, Commanding Colored Brigade, Norfolk, Va.:

SIR: Probably no expedition, during the progress of this war, has been attended with more utter disregard for the long-established usages of civilization or the dictates of humanity, than your late raid into the country bordering the Albemarle. Your stay, though short, was marked by crimes and enormities. You burned houses over the heads of defenseless women and children, carried off private property of every description, arrested non-combatants, and carried off ladies in irons, whom you confined with negro men.

Your negro troops fired on confederates after they had surrendered, and they were only saved by the exertions of the more humane of your white officers. Last, but not least, under the pretext that he was a guerrilla, you hanged Daniel Bright, a private of company L, Sixty-second Georgia regiment, (cavalry,) forcing the ladies and gentlemen whom you held in arrest to witness the execution. Therefore, I have obtained an order from the General Commanding, for the

execution of Samuel Jones, a private of company B, Fifth Ohio, whom
I hang in retaliation. I hold two more of your men—in irons—as
hostages for Mrs. Weeks and Mrs. Mundin. When these ladies are
released, these men will be relieved and treated as prisoners of war.

JOEL R. GRIFFIN, *Colonel.*

IV

NEGRO TROOPS MEET THE CONFEDERATES IN BATTLE

Fort Pillow in Tennessee, near the Kentucky border, had been a Confederate
defense, but early in the summer of 1862, Union forces had captured it. The
Confederate general, Nathan Bedford Forrest, a former slavedealer from
Memphis, began an assault to regain the fort in April 1864, and in a letter to
Lieutenant Colonel Thomas M. Jack, he described the battle. ☐ *Official
Records, War of the Rebellion.* Washington: U.S. Government Printing Office,
p. 610.

HEADQUARTERS FORREST'S CAVALRY
JACKSON, TENN., April 15, 1864

COLONEL: A dispatch of the 9th instant from the lieutenant-
general commanding reached me on the morning of the 13th at Fort
Pillow. Have dispatched by telegraph of the capture of Fort
Pillow. . . .

Arrived there on the morning of the 12th and attacked the place
with a portion of McCulloch's and Bell's brigades, numbering about
1,500 men, and after a sharp contest captured the garrison and all of
its stores. A demand was made for the surrender, which was refused.
The victory was complete, and the loss of the enemy will never be
known from the fact that large numbers ran into the river and were
shot and drowned. The force was composed of about 500 negroes and
200 white soldiers (Tennessee Tories). The river was dyed with the
blood of the slaughtered for 200 yards. There was in the fort a large
number of citizens who had fled there to escape the conscript law.
Most of these ran into the river and were drowned.

The approximate loss was upward of 500 killed, but few of the
officers escaping.

It is hoped that these facts will demonstrate to the Northern
people that negro soldiers cannot cope with Southerners. We still
hold the fort. . . .

N. B. FORREST, *Major-General, Commanding.*

The capture of Fort Pillow by the Confederates and the huge loss of life among Union soldiers was considered a massacre in the North, and the battle became the subject of a federal investigation. In his testimony, a Union cavalryman, William J. Mays, gave an account of the surrender of the fort. □ *Official Records, War of the Rebellion,* pp. 525–526.

I was at Fort Pillow on the 12th of April, 1864, and engaged in the fight there. . . . Two assaults were made by them [the enemy], and both repulsed. This was about 11 or 12 a.m., when a flag of truce was sent in demanding a surrender. While the flag was being received and the firing suspended the enemy were moving their forces into position. . . .

In about five minutes after the disappearance of the flag of truce a general assault was made upon our works from every direction. They were kept at bay for some time, when the negroes gave way upon the left and ran down the bluff, leaving an opening through which the rebels entered and immediately commenced an indiscriminate slaughter of both white and black. We all threw down our arms and gave tokens of surrender, asking for quarter (I was wounded in the right shoulder and muscle of the back and knocked down before I threw down my gun). But no quarter was given. Voices were heard upon all sides, crying, "Give them no quarter; kill them; kill them; it is General Forrest's orders." I saw 4 white men and at least 25 negroes shot while begging for mercy, and I saw 1 negro dragged from a hollow log within 10 feet of where I lay, and as 1 rebel held him by the foot another shot him. These were all soldiers. There were also 2 negro women and 3 little children standing within 25 steps from me, when a rebel stepped up to them and . . . shot them all. . . . They [the Confederate soldiers] then disappeared in the direction of the landing, following up the fugitives, firing at them wherever seen. They came back in about three-quarters of an hour, shooting and robbing the dead of their money and clothes. I saw a man with a canteen upon him and a pistol in his hand. I ventured to ask him for a drink of water. He turned around . . . and shot at my head three different times, covering my face with dust, and then turned from me — no doubt thinking he had killed me . . . . I lay there until dark, feigning death, when a rebel officer came along, drawing his saber, and ordered me to get up, threatening to run his saber into me if I did not, saying I had to march 10 miles that night. I succeeded in getting up and got among a small squad he had already gathered up, but stole away from them during the night . . . .

A fellow officer of General Forrest, John A. Wyeth, was also his biographer. Wyeth had served under the general but not at Fort Pillow. His comments on the ordeal express his views thirty years after the battle at the fort. ☐ John Allan Wyeth, M.D. *Life of General Nathan Bedford Forrest.* New York and London: Harper & Brothers, 1899, pp. 367–368.

There can be little doubt, however, that it was the heavy loss of life—the unusually large proportion of killed and wounded to the number of soldiers engaged, which led to the report of the Committee of Congress, and caused this engagement to pass into history as the "Fort Pillow Massacre."

To the rational mind, capable of carefully weighing the evidence on both sides, and arriving at a conclusion unbiased by prejudice, it must be clear that there was no massacre as charged. Had a wholesale and merciless slaughter been intended by General Forrest and his subordinates, it could and would have been carried out, as there was nothing to prevent it. The fact that so many escaped death is of itself a proof that a massacre was not premeditated or permitted. It is true that more of the garrison were shot after the Southern troops were in possession of the breastworks than was necessary for the full success of the assault, but under the conditions which prevailed during the attack, it is clearly shown that an unusually large loss in killed and wounded was inevitable, even had no excesses been indulged in by the captors.

From a careful study of the subject, I am convinced that a few desperate or insanely intoxicated soldiers of the garrison resisted to the very last, and even after escape was hopeless continued to fire at the Confederates. On the other hand, notwithstanding this extreme provocation, there were a number of men, both white and black, shot down, who were trying to surrender and should have been spared. About an hour before the assault was made a detachment of Forrest's command posted at the extreme left of his line broke into the quarter-master's stores which had been captured at this time, and before they could be compelled to quit the building had had access to a supply of whiskey which they discovered there. The moment Forrest learned that his men were pillaging the captured stores he rode there rapidly and put a stop to it in person.

The incidents, however, which did occur were greatly exaggerated and cleverly distorted in the reports. In extracting the testimony, the committee, for political purposes, and as part of an important war measure, gave a bloody coloring to the whole. Everything considered, it may well be a matter of surprise that the slaughter was not greater. Human life was held exceedingly cheap in 1864, and especially in west Tennessee; the scenes of bloodshed which stained this section of the South may well suggest the reddest days of the French Revolution.

It is difficult for those who did not live through this unhappy period, and in this immediate section, to appreciate the bitterness of feeling which then prevailed. Three years of civil war had passed, not without a deplorable effect upon the morals of the rank and file of either army. War does not bring out the noblest traits in the majority of those who from choice or necessity follow its blood-stained paths. Too often the better qualities hide away, and those that are harsh and cruel prevail. Some of Forrest's men treasured a deep resentment against some of the officers and soldiers of this garrison. They had been neighbors in times of peace, and had taken opposite sides when the war came on. These men had suffered violence to person and property, and their wives and children, in the enforced absence of their natural protectors, had suffered various indignities at the hands of the "Tennessee Tories," as the loyal Tennesseeans were called by their neighbors who sided with the South. When they met in single combat, or in scouting parties, or in battle, as far as these individuals were concerned, it was too often a duel to the death. Between the parties to these neighborhood feuds the laws of war did not prevail. Here, in this mêlée, in the fire and excitement of the assault, they found opportunity and made excuse for bloody vengeance.

PROBLEM 5

The Freedmen's Bureau During Reconstruction

When the Civil War ended in 1865, the South not only experienced the bitterness of defeat, but faced a drastic change in its way of living. Thousands of slaves had escaped from their owners during the course of the war, and the work of finding employment, food, and shelter for such a multitude fell to the lot of military officers and private agencies. Finally, in March 1865, Congress established the Bureau of Refugees, Freedmen, and Abandoned Lands, commonly known as the Freedmen's Bureau. The Bureau was to last for the rest of the war and for one year thereafter. General Oliver O. Howard, who had marched through Georgia with Sherman, was named commissioner.

During 1865 and 1866, governments of Southern states (formed under President Johnson's Reconstruction program) passed vagrancy and apprenticeship laws that bound Negroes to the land on which they worked and controlled ways in which they might conduct themselves. To counteract these laws, or Black Codes, Congress enlarged the powers and extended the term of the Freedmen's Bureau. During its existence, the Bureau aided the poor, established schools, provided hospitals, medical aid, food, and clothing for Negroes and destitute whites. It also furnished financial aid to Fisk, Howard, Berea, and Atlanta colleges, which were established during the Reconstruction period. Its accomplishments were highly praised by some people, but the Bureau was also severely criticized by others for its wide political influence and for its poor choice of agents. Of all Reconstruction measures, many Southerners considered the Freedmen's Bureau the most corrupt and unjust. They resented it even more than the series of Reconstruction acts passed by Congress in 1867, which demanded new qualifications of the states for readmission to the Union, enfranchised Negroes, and deprived many Confederate leaders of voting rights.

Problem 5 deals with the controversial Freedmen's Bureau, whose main work ended in 1869. In reading, consider the following questions:

1 In the Ku Klux reports, what were the main criticisms of the Freedmen's Bureau?

2 Does the description of the activities of a Freedmen's Bureau agent indicate shortcomings as well as the effectiveness of the Bureau? Explain.

3 What characteristics of the Freedmen's Bureau does Coulter emphasize? Franklin? What are basic points of disagreement between the two historians?

4 From these readings, would you say that the Bureau was a success or a failure? Give evidence for your conclusion.

I

CRITICISM OF THE FREEDMEN'S BUREAU

The following excerpts were selected from testimony given before Congressional committees investigating conditions in the South during 1870 and 1871.
□ Walter L. Fleming. *Documentary History of Reconstruction*, Volume I. Cleveland: The Arthur H. Clark Company, 1907. Pp. 373–374, 369, 371, 372.

Ku Klux Report (1871). Views of the minority.

First, as to the Freedmen's Bureau and its operations. By this act, four millions of negroes became the pupils, wards, servitors, and pliant tools of a political and extremely partisan agency, inimical and deadly hostile to the peace, order, and best interests of southern society. Under the workings of the Reconstruction and Freedmen's

Bureau acts the foundations of social and political order were uprooted and overturned; the former master became the slave, and the former slave became the master, the elector, the law-maker, and the ostensible ruler. The agents of the Freedmen's Bureau were, as we have shown before, generally of a class of fanatics without character or responsibility . . . . It was a common practice, after a planter or farmer had contracted in the required form with the freedmen for the year, had his crops planted and in process of cultivation, that his negro laborers would suddenly *strike* for higher wages. Nothing but the intervention of the Bureau agent could induce them to return, and that *inducement* could only be effected by the planter or farmer paying to the agent from ten to twenty dollars per head. This sum was simply *a perquisite* of the agent, and when paid, the negro always returned to his labors, though not receiving a cent of additional compensation. It was frequently the case that the same planter or farmer would have to compensate the Bureau agent from *two to three times during one year, or lose his crops.* This system of ingenious blackmailing produced no little irritation, and frequently total bankruptcy of the planter.

Ku Klux Report, Alabama Testimony (1871). Statement of A. D. Sayre, formerly a Whig:
When the agents first came there . . . they established a Freedmen's Bureau. They notified everybody that they must employ their freedmen, and that all contracts must be submitted to the inspection of the Freedmen's Bureau; that no man would be allowed to employ freedmen unless their contracts were submitted to and approved by that Bureau. . . . They listened to every sort of tale that any dissatisfied negro might choose to tell; they would send out and arrest white men, bring them in under guard, try them, and put them in jail. They got hold of plantations there, what they called refuges for freedmen. It was announced that if the freedmen got dissatisfied they could enter there, and be fed and clothed, and taken care of. In that way large numbers of negroes were enticed away from plantations where they had been living, and they flocked to these places. Hundreds of them died from neglect. The impression was produced upon the negro that the white man who had been his master was his enemy, and that these men [Freedmen Bureau agents] were his peculiar friends; that they had nothing to expect . . through their old masters.

II

ACTIVITIES OF A FREEDMEN'S BUREAU AGENT

An article that appeared in the *New York Tribune* for February 3, 1866 describes the work performed by Captain Glavis, a Freedmen's Bureau agent. The article was included in the Report of Joint Committee on Reconstruction in 1866. ☐ Walter L. Fleming, ed. *Documents Relating to Reconstruction.* Morgantown, West Virginia: 1904. Pp. 52–53.

Captain Glavis . . . visits each county at least once a week. There is no civil law, and he has to act as judge, jury, magistrate, sheriff, and everything else in these six counties. . . . Yesterday was court day in Wilson county, and at the captain's invitation I accompanied him. After breakfast the captain, with the assistance of two clerks, began his court. There were about five hundred people of all colors and classes waiting for a hearing. They come in, state their cases, and are disposed of in quick order; it taking all day, however, to get through. . . . The negroes generally come to get hired out, or bound out if under age, to make complaint against their former masters for wages retained, for rations, and the settlement of all disputes. Rations are rarely given except in very urgent cases; and no negro can make complaint to the Bureau unless he or she had made some contract for support for the ensuing year. This is a good rule, and compels the unwilling and lazy to work. Thus, you see, all the stuff about the Freedmen's Bureau being a refuge for indolent negroes is so much falsehood. All contracts for labor are made through the bureau, or else they are not valid in case of a disagreement between the parties. Consequently there are always a large number of planters constantly besieging the bureau for laborers. Yesterday Captain Glavis signed no less than forty contracts between planters and negroes. The contracts . . . set forth the duties and requirements of each party. The most important one is that the employer shall do all in his power to promote the establishment of schools for the employe's children. Quite a number of children are bound out also. Most of the complaints yesterday were made by negroes against their former masters for wages. . . . A couple of negroes brought complaint against an old planter, a former master, for wages. Planter was ordered for trial, the case was heard, and it was clearly proven that the negroes were entitled to their wages.

III

ASSESSMENTS OF THE FREEDMEN'S BUREAU

Reconstruction ended in 1877. Seventy years later, a Southern historian wrote a description of the period in the "spirit of the times," attempting to avoid judgment of the South. In this selection, he gives his views of the Freedmen's Bureau. ☐ From *The South During Reconstruction, 1865–1877* by E. Merton Coulter. Copyright 1947. Reprinted by permission of Louisiana State University Press. Pp. 70, 74, 75, 76, 89-91.

The Bureau entered the laudable field of providing the freedman a job as a free laborer and seeking to protect his rights as a worker. If this supervision had been carried out by people who knew as much about Negroes and conditions in the South as did the Southerners, there should have been no complaint; but the supervising agents were largely Northern placemen [political appointees] and former Federal soldiers. Though not uniformly visionary, many of them were enough so to bring down upon themselves the opposition not only of planters but even of some of the freedmen. During the war Negroes had been forced by Federal armies to labor on seized plantations and some of the rules used were adopted after the war both by the Freedmen's Bureau and by the planters.

Southerners, knowing Negroes better, felt that they should be allowed to deal with the freedmen without interference. De Bow declared that when he was superintendent of the Census in 1850 he made a study of free Negroes, and that he found them "immeasurably better off" in the South than in the North. Free Negroes, therefore, offered no new problem. "The best friend today that the freedman has," said a Southern editor, "is the Southern man.". . .

Continuing to work on the same plantations for the same masters appeared to the freedmen too much like slavery, and as long as they could go to town and get Bureau rations they expected to enjoy their freedom. They did not like to be summoned to work by the old slave devices of blaring horns and clanging bells and they did not like the term "overseer" any longer. And some of them began to dislike their old friend King Cotton. Said one, "If ole massa want to grow cotton, let him plant it himself. I'se work for him dese twenty years, and done got nothin' but food and clothes, and dem mighty mean; now I'se freedman, and I tell you I ain't going to work cotton *no*how." To protect himself and the freedman, too, the planter as well as the Freedmen's Bureau, insisted on written contracts, but the freedman not always understanding them and soon forgetting what he might have understood did not like to sign them. He wanted to be a free agent to take advantage of any opportunity which might come his way; never having had a chance heretofore, he could not well be blamed for wanting to seize any flood tide that might come along. Now having something which the planter must have, he could use his labor as a club to be swung in many directions. . . .

The Freedmen's Bureau had a fundamentally important task to perform in the South, of more personal consequence to the inhabitants, black and white, than the political and constitutional reconstructing which so thoroughly engaged the attention of Congress. It could have given a trend to race relations which would have helped to solve a problem made for the South when the first Negroes were landed in Jamestown. In this most fundamental of all Southern problems it made a conspicuous failure. It worked to bring about suspicion which ripened into racial hostility. While Radical Reconstruction was in the making, many Bureau commissioners and agents acted as spies and representatives of the Congressional leaders; and when elections under this new Reconstruction were held, many who had been connected with the Bureau reached office. . . . Thus was a farce played upon representative government; these Northerners could not represent the South, for, as a Northern newspaper stated, they were "mere representatives of New York or New England interests."

Apart from a few assistant commissioners the personnel of the Bureau was susceptible to charges of personal dishonesty and corruption. Even General Howard himself was not above reproach, and although committees of investigation exonerated him, it could not be successfully denied that his records were carelessly kept, that he was lax in carrying out the law, and that his use of Bureau funds was not always correct. Distrustful of the Bureau activities from the beginning, President Johnson appointed Generals James B. Steedman and A. R. Fullerton to make an investigation. . . . They found the agent at Newbern, North Carolina, exercising the "most arbitrary and despotic power" and "practicing revolting and unheard-of cruelties on the helpless freedmen under his charge." The law allowed agents to rent for themselves abandoned lands, on which they worked the freedmen and frequently cheated them out of their wages or part of the crops. Generals Steedman and Fullerton declared that some of the agents taught the freedmen "to distrust all white men but those who had immediate authority over them," and "under the guise of friendship, took advantage of their credulity, and fraudulently appropriated their crops." The agents were notorious in appropriating fines and forfeitures for their own use. Steedman and Fullerton believed a special investigator could find in every state "*stealings*, which in our opinion are very large." The meanest villainy was to foment freedmen strikes in the busiest period of the season, and settle the trouble at $20 a head, with the result that the Negroes would be forced to return to work at the same wage and the agents would pocket the fees. Well might the Negroes themselves cry out against their friends and protectors. John Wallace, a Florida Negro, said of the Bureau: "Instead of a blessing it proved the worse curse of the race." Southerners long remembered and detested this organization with its agents, hangers-on, and schoolmarm teachers . . . .

In this selection, John Hope Franklin, a Negro historian, explains why he believes that the Freedmen's Bureau gained "a notable success in ministering to human welfare."   ☐ From FROM SLAVERY TO FREEDOM, Third Edition, by John Hope Franklin. Copyright 1947, © 1956, 1967 by Alfred A. Knopf, Inc. Reprinted by permission of the publisher. Pp. 306 – 309

In the closing months of the war and afterwards the South suffered acutely. The abandoned lands, the want of food and clothing, the thousands of displaced persons, and the absence of organized civil authority to cope with the emergency merely suggest the nature of the suffering. The extent of it among both Negroes and whites can scarcely be imagined. Negroes were distressed not only because they lacked the necessaries of life but also because they genuinely feared, especially after the death of President Lincoln, that they would gradually slip back into a condition hardly better than that of slaves. In the summer and fall of 1865 they held several conventions, all looking toward an improvement of their conditions. A Negro convention in Nashville protested seating the Tennessee delegation to Congress because the legislature had not passed just laws for Negroes. It also demanded that Congress recognize Negro citizenship. A group of 120, meeting in Raleigh, North Carolina, declared that they wanted fair wages, education for their children, and repeal of the discriminatory laws passed by the state legislature. Mississippi Negroes protested against reactionary policies in their state and asked Congress to extend the franchise to Negroes. It was the same thing in Charleston and Mobile: Negroes were demanding suffrage, the abolition of Black Codes, and measures for the relief of suffering.

While the pleas of Negroes were largely ignored in the South, there were Northerners who worked to relieve their distress. Private organizations had taken up this work during the war, and considerable pressure was applied to Congress as early as 1863 to assume responsibility for the welfare of needy whites and Negroes in the South. Military commanders did whatever they could or wanted to do with regard to relief.

The need, however, was for a comprehensive and unified service for freedmen. It was not until March, 1865, that the Bureau of Refugees, Freedmen, and Abandoned Lands, better known as the Freedmen's Bureau, was established. With officials in each of the Southern states, the Bureau aided refugees and freedmen by furnishing supplies and medical services, establishing schools, supervising contracts between freedmen and their employers, and managing confiscated or abandoned lands, leasing and selling some of them to freedmen.

The atmosphere in which the Freedmen's Bureau worked was one of hostility. Many Northerners looked upon it as an expensive agency, the existence of which could not be justified in times of peace. In the South the opposition to the Bureau was vehement. There was serious objection to federal interference with the relations between the worker and his employer. It was believed, moreover, that the Bureau had a political program for enfranchising the Negro and establishing a strong Republican party in the South.

There can be no doubt that the Freedmen's Bureau relieved much suffering among Negroes and whites. Between 1865 and 1869, for example, the Bureau issued twenty-one million rations, approximately five million going to whites and fifteen million to Negroes. By 1867 there were 46 hospitals under the Bureau staffed with physicians, surgeons, and nurses. The medical department spent over two million dollars to improve the health of freedmen, and treated more than 450,000 cases of illness. The death rate among freedmen was reduced, and sanitary conditions were improved.

The Bureau undertook to resettle many people who had been displaced during the war. Because of the urgent need for labor to cultivate the land, free transportation was furnished freedmen to leave congested areas and to become self-supporting. By 1870 more than 30,000 persons had been moved. Although abandoned and confiscated lands were generally restored to their owners under the amnesty proclamations of Lincoln and Johnson, the Bureau distributed some land to freedmen. Colonies of infirm, destitute, and vagrant Negroes were set up in several states. Small parcels of land were first alloted and then leased to them for management and cultivation.

The Bureau sought to protect the Negro in his freedom to choose his own employer and to work at a fair wage. Both parties were required to live up to their contract. Agents of the Bureau consulted with planters and freedmen, urging the former to be fair in their dealings, and instructing the latter in the necessity of working to provide for their families and to achieve independence and security. Thousands of Negroes returned to work under conditions more satisfactory than those which had existed before the Bureau supervised their relations with employers. General Oliver Otis Howard reported that "in a single state not less than fifty thousand such [labor] contracts were drawn." Paul S. Pierce[1] has estimated that in the South as a whole there must have been several hundred thousand contracts.

When it was felt that the interest of Negroes could not be safely entrusted to local courts, the Bureau organized freedmen's courts and boards of arbitration. They had civil and criminal jurisdiction over minor cases where one or both parties were freedmen. Frequently an expression of the Bureau's interest was sufficient to secure justice for freedmen in the regular courts. In Maryland, for example, the case of a white physician who assaulted a Negro without provocation was carried by the Bureau agent to the state supreme court, which admitted the Negro's testimony and convicted the physician.

The Bureau achieved its greatest success in education. It set up or supervised all kinds of schools: day, night, Sunday, and industrial schools, as well as colleges. It cooperated closely with philanthropic and religious organizations in the North in the establishment of many institutions. Among the schools founded in this period which received aid from the Bureau were Howard University, Hampton Institute, St. Augustine's College, Atlanta University, Fisk University, Storer College, and Biddle Memorial Institute (now Johnson C. Smith University). The American Missionary Association, the Baptists, Methodists, Presbyterians, and Episcopalians were all active in establishing schools. Education was promoted so vigorously that by 1867

[1]Author of *The Freedmen's Bureau, A Chapter in the History of Reconstruction* (Iowa City, 1904).

schools had been set up in "the remotest counties of each of the confederate states."

Teachers came down from the North in large numbers. Besides Edmund Ware at Atlanta, Samuel C. Armstrong at Hampton, and Erastus M. Cravath at Fisk, there were hundreds whose services were not as widely known. In 1869 there were 9,503 teachers in the freedmen's schools of the South. Although some were Southerners, a majority of the whites came from the North. The number of Negro teachers was growing; and gradually they took over supervision of some schools.

By 1870, when the educational work of the Bureau stopped, there were 247,333 pupils in 4,329 schools. Reports from all quarters "showed a marked increase in attendance, and advance in scholarship, and a record of punctuality and regularity which compared favorably with the schools in the north." The Bureau had spent more than five million dollars in schooling Negroes. The shortcomings in their education arose not from a want of zeal on the part of teachers but from ignorance of the needs of Negroes and from the necessary preoccupation of students with the problem of survival in a hostile world.

Despite Southern hostility to the Bureau, and the inefficiency of many officials, it performed a vastly important task during Reconstruction. As a relief agency it deserves to be ranked with the great efforts of recent depressions and wars. It demonstrated that the government could administer an extensive program of relief and rehabilitation, and suggested a way in which the nation could grapple with its pressing social problems. To be sure, there was corruption and inefficiency, but not enough to prevent the Bureau from achieving a notable success in ministering to human welfare.

PROBLEM 6

The South and Jim Crow

Someone once referred to the South as the "Land of the Epidermis where every white person was a little king." In the late nineteenth and early twentieth centuries, skin color was truly crucial to one's existence. It determined how one lived, learned, worked, and died. This system of racial segregation, which had begun with slavery and had been strengthened by the post-Civil War Black Codes, was established legally by one Southern state after another between 1890 and 1917. It had as its avowed purpose the maintenance of white supremacy. No black man was ever to attain a position as high as that of the lowest white.

Between 1890 and 1917, therefore, state and local laws defined carefully the place the Negro was to have in Southern life. In all areas where the races might meet as social equals, there was to be separation. Fear of social equality—"how would you like your daughter to marry one of them?"—helped to create the color line which marked off restaurants, theaters, beaches, saloons, schools, courts, and cemeteries. "Jim Crow," the name given to discriminatory legislation in 1875, took on new meaning: Jim Crow Bibles to swear on in Atlanta courts; Jim Crow cemeteries for dogs in Washington; Jim Crow text-books in Florida.

What had become of those liberals in the North who had right-eously demanded equal rights for the Negro? By 1900, they were silent. C. Vann Woodward, in *The Strange Career of Jim Crow*, pointed out that the North gave the South "permission to hate" the Negro. The Northern press, in the main, ceased criticizing Southern treatment of Negroes. Federal courts began to hand down decisions which permitted segregation. As early as 1883, the Supreme Court declared the Civil Rights Act unconstitutional; thirteen years later, the Court ruled that "separate but equal" facilities for the Negro were constitutional. Northerners, tired of the Negro problem and eager to conciliate the South, left the solution of the nagging problem in the hands of those who "knew the Negro best." In short, the South was free to deal with the Negro as it saw fit. For a time after Reconstruction white Southerners were uncertain as to what the Negro's place should be. Rival political parties and factions at first fought to attract Negro voters, but then decided to exclude Negroes from politics altogether by denying them the vote. Even the Populists, who undertook a strik-ing program of racial cooperation in politics during the severe agri-cultural depression of the 1890's, yielded to the temptations of racial prejudice and consented to Negro disfranchisement.

Of course, social separation and discrimination had existed long before this period. The force of Southern custom, threats of violence, and social etiquette continued to remind the Negro of his inferior position. A Negro was rarely called "mister"; "boy," "uncle," or "auntie" was sufficient. Lynchings, whippings, and beatings were common treatment for "uppity" Negroes. By the time of World War I, law had combined with custom to specify for the Negro an inferior position in Southern life.

The readings for Problem 6 will explore white and Negro atti-tudes toward Jim Crow. Both Negroes and whites speak their minds on the system of superiority-inferiority relationships. It is well to remember that no attempt has been made to cover the full range of attitudes. The reader should realize that there were some whites who objected to the degrading effects of the racial-etiquette system as well as some Negroes who made no special objection to it. As you read the selections, consider the following questions:

1 Why was there segregation, according to the whites who were interviewed?

2   Rationalizations are excuses. Can you find examples of people rationalizing the existence of segregation? Cite evidence.

3   Compare the arguments used by the Southern whites with those used by the Ohio legislators in Problem 3 and with the account of the English traveler in Problem 2. Are any of these arguments similar? What conclusion can be reached?

4   From Richard Wright's account, what impact did Jim Crow have on the Negro? How was the Negro psychologically affected? Was the white affected also? How?

I

INTERVIEWS WITH WHITE SOUTHERNERS

Maurine Boie, a white sociologist, interviewed a cross section of the white population from Maine to Louisiana, including some parts of the Midwest, on racial attitudes. The following excerpts express views of some people interviewed. □ *Racial Attitudes.* Social Science Source Documents, No. 3. Social Science Institute, Fisk University. Nashville, Tenn.: Fisk University, 1946, pp. 140–141, 144, 168, 170, 187, 189.

Subject: Male   Occupation: City Official
Age: 40   Residence: Charleston, S. C.

I was a country boy and raised on a plantation. . . . My observation is that my kind attitude is but a continuation of that of my father and mother. No man ever had a father who did more for his colored workers. Being thrown with them thus intimately, and doing all kinds of work along with them, I had as intimate contact as any man could. In all these associations there was a very decided and definite line drawn, which was never crossed except in very rare instances. Because I believe that with the white man in power . . . absolute justice to Negroes should be noticed in every instance, in fact a kind justice. . . . At the same time that does not suggest racial equality; that is preposterous and abhorrent and would not be tolerated in the South for one second. It's not a good thing for the colored race. God made us two races. Social equality would be but one step removed from intermarriage – a mongrel race. The secret of the English race is that it has never permitted any contamination of its blood stream. That is why England is such a superior country.

The colored man may be good for some reason beyond my comprehension, but I don't believe God expected them to mix with us. The white man has been the civilizer. . . . He has demonstrated his ability to lead. Why experiment with the abilities of other races?

We, of the South, would spend the last drop of our blood before we would submit to the domination, dictation, or social affiliation on the line of equality with colored men. That is just as fixed as the stars and all the education in the world won't change it. I did much work among the colored folk as a lawyer and a judge. I used keen insight to study them from that angle. That experience finally attained results in the feeling that this is a white man's country and will remain so. . . . The idea of slavery is abhorrent. Slavery certainly didn't help the South; it has pauperized it. . . . We are kind and considerate and just to them in the main, but they are never permitted to cross the social invisible line between the races. That is now, has been and ever shall be there. In the North they are permitted to believe they are equal. They try their fancy stuff here and get their brains knocked out. . . .

Subject: Female   Occupation: Housewife
Age: 40   Residence: Greensboro, N. C.

I came here when the Negro was a menace, so I can't quite recover from my prejudice. As a Negro he is the most lovable creature in the world, but you have to keep him at a distance to seem so. I have analysed him carefully and I can get along as well as anyone with my servants. Its not hard to. They are as lovable as anyone in a lower order of life could be. They can never reach the same level of superiority with white people.

They know what real courtesy is. This morning I was asleep when the milkman came. He could have gotten in as we never lock the doors but he came back later because the dog was always so noisy when he saw him and he didn't want to disturb me. I shall always feel that the Negro ought to come to the back door. I cannot see that they are fitted for university education. Whether education spoils them is a question. We have a Negro college with a colored man at the head. . . . He is tolerant, makes no assumptions for himself; he teaches them that there are certain things which they have and they must develop them and not be imitators. He is a lovable leader. If we weren't prejudiced we would think he should associate with the educated people in the town.

Subject: Male   Occupation: Chief mechanic,
                                                     Railroad shops
Age: 45   Residence: Macon, Georgia

The niggers here are simply a different class of people. . . .
In the South he is treated as a nigger and is at home here. He knows
this treatment is the best for him. He knows he can come to an old
southern family and get what he wants. Their living standards are
much below ours; they can get along on half what a white man can.
. . . They don't try to take advantage of us. We always make separate provisions for them.

We have six hundred colored workers here. We accord them the
same treatment as the white people. But they know enough to take
off their hats and humble themselves before white people.

I had a case not long ago of a nigger who couldn't bury his mother
because he didn't have enough money. I wrote to the undertaker and
told him he'd get his money each week and so they had the funeral.
They appreciate that kind of thing. We are too young to know about
slavery, but we have heard our ancestors speak of it. Then we were
raised right with them and knew they were servants. They were just
like part of the family but were to do whatever the white man told
them. I liked the little nigger boys to play with; they would do just
what we told them to.

We feel toward them like the affection one has for a dog; we
love 'em in their place. But he stays in his place. . . .

Sometimes we have to keep them there. They are like a herd of
sheep. We have a good group around here. It's years and years since
we've had a lynching. It's not necessary to lynch them. The sheriffs
in this county take more care of the darky than the white man. We
have pretty good feeling here on the whole. They respect the white
race for they know white people will treat them fairly. When one gets
into trouble he appeals to a white man, not to one of his own race.

We hardly have such a thing as a Negro voting. They wouldn't
vote if you gave them a chance. A few do in the general election.
They are not interested; they know it's not part of their social life.

There's no problem between the two races. The Negro gets
justice with equal opportunities in every way. They have fine schools,
kept up by the same board of education, etc. The county hospitals
have wards for them just like for the white people. Nine-tenths of the
charity work done in the county is for colored people. They are well-
provided for everywhere.

Subject: Male   Occupation: Minister
                                  Residence: Waycross, Georgia

I believe that the Negro should have equality before the law, economically, of every type except social. I should never come to a time when I invite one as an equal into my home, when I introduce my wife in a social way to be the friend of a colored man. That's based primarily on the conception fundamental in my mind and generally accepted that intermarriage is something to be frowned upon and resented. As a means to that, the line must be drawn on social equality. It's not social subjection but social separation that ought to be encouraged and aided in every possible development on all lines. I spoke to them just last Sunday. I told them every family should have commodious, neat, comfortable homes; that we all needed better homes; that I would be delighted to see them dress better, to see them successful, etc. I believe in encouraging their own businesses, professions, lodges, churches, etc. One of the greatest means of assuming friendliness between the races is ownership of property. It gives them a feeling of responsibility. They should be encouraged to the limit and to build up their own social life of a high and proper sort, but the line between the races must be drawn and the best Negro leaders agree to that. They realize that the lack of social mixing doesn't imply inequality or inferiority. In the practical working out of the Negro and white woman, although they have good friendships, wonderful family loyalties based on common work and trust, they never shake hands with each other. . . . We feel toward them like we do about our pets. I would hate awfully to have a black skin. My son made up as a Negro comedian one day and couldn't get the color off. He asked an old Negro man how he stood it being black all the time. The old man said he would like mighty much to have a white skin. I thought it was so pathetic. But I think they are coming to value their own race. They do imitate—that's their strongest trait. . . . They are gradually becoming more proud, in their attitude toward themselves, I mean, not impudent toward white people. They seem more contented. . . . They have a pleasant attitude [toward] each other. I went to a vocal contest in a colored church; they have charming manners. . . . Some of the Negroes have lovely eyes, etc; though I couldn't think one was really beautiful. A bad-mannered, impudent Negro is the worst thing on earth. They attach their sense of inferiority to it and its awful. I try to forget their foolishness.

II

EXPERIENCES OF A SOUTHERN NEGRO

Richard Wright, a Negro novelist, tells about some of his experiences when he was a boy in Mississippi. ☐ From *Black Boy* by Richard Wright. Copyright 1937, 1942, 1944, 1945 by Richard Wright. Reprinted by permission of Harper & Row, Publishers and Jonathan Cape Ltd. Pp. 158–161 passim.

The store owned a bicycle which I used in delivering purchases. One day, while returning from the suburbs, my bicycle tire was punctured. I walked along the hot, dusty road, sweating and leading the bicycle by the handle bars.

A car slowed at my side.

"What's the matter there, boy?" a white man called.

I told him that my bicycle was broken and that I was walking back to town.

"That's too bad," he said. "Hop on the running board."

He stopped the car. I clutched hard at my bicycle with one hand and clung to the side of the car with the other.

"All set?"

"Yes, sir."

The car started. It was full of young white men. They were drinking. I watched the flask pass from mouth to mouth.

"Wanna drink, boy?" one asked. . . .

"Oh, no!" I said.

The words were barely out of my mouth before I felt something hard and cold smash me between the eyes. It was an empty whisky bottle. I saw stars, and fell backwards from the speeding car into the dust of the road, my feet becoming entangled in the steel spokes of the bicycle. The car stopped and the white men piled out and stood over me.

"Nigger, ain't you learned no better sense'n that yet?" asked the man who hit me. "Ain't you learned to say *sir* to a white man yet?"

Dazed, I pulled to my feet. My elbows and legs were bleeding. Fists doubled, the white man advanced, kicking the bicycle out of the way. "Aw, leave . . . [him] alone. He's got enough," said one.

They stood looking at me. I rubbed my shins, trying to stop the flow of blood. No doubt they felt a sort of contemptuous pity, for one asked:

"You wanna ride to town now, nigger? You reckon you know enough to ride now?"

"I wanna walk," I said simply.

Maybe I sounded funny. They laughed.

"Well, walk, you black . . . !"

Before they got back into their car, they comforted me with:

"Nigger, you sure ought to be glad it was us you talked to that way. You're . . . lucky . . . 'cause if you'd said that to some other white man, you might've been a dead nigger now."

I was learning rapidly how to watch white people, to observe their every move, every fleeting expression, how to interpret what was said and what left unsaid.

Late one Saturday night I made some deliveries in a white neighborhood. I was pedaling my bicycle back to the store as fast as I could when a police car, swerving toward me, jammed me into the curbing.

"Get down, nigger, and put up your hands!" they ordered.

I did. They climbed out of the car, guns drawn, faces set, and advanced slowly.

"Keep still!" they ordered.

I reached my hands higher. They searched my pockets and packages. They seemed dissatisfied when they could find nothing incriminating. Finally, one of them said:

"Boy, tell your boss not to send you out in white neighborhoods at this time of night."

"Yes, sir," I said.

I rode off, feeling that they might shoot at me, feeling that the pavement might disappear. It was like living in a dream, the reality of which might change at any moment. . . .

I held a series of petty jobs for short periods, quitting some to work elsewhere, being driven off others because of my attitude, my speech, the look in my eyes. I was no nearer than ever to my goal of saving enough money to leave. At times I doubted if I could ever do it.

One jobless morning I went to my old classmate, Griggs, who worked for a Capitol Street jeweler. He was washing the windows of the store when I came upon him.

"Do you know where I can find a job?" I asked.

He looked at me with scorn.

"Yes, I know where you can find a job," he said, laughing.

"Where?"

"But I wonder if you can hold it," he said.

"What do you mean?" I asked. "Where's the job?"

"Take your time," he said. "You know, Dick, I know you. You've been trying to hold a job all summer, and you can't. Why? Because you're impatient. That's your big fault."

I said nothing, because he was repeating what I had already heard him say. He lit a cigarette and blew out smoke leisurely.

"Well," I said, egging him on to speak.

"I wish to hell I could talk to you," he said.

"I think I know what you want to tell me," I said.

He clapped me on the shoulder; his face was full of fear, hate, concern for me.

"Do you want to get killed?" he asked me.

"Hell, no!"

"Then, for God's sake, learn how to live in the South!"

"What do you mean?" I demanded. "Let white people tell me that. Why should you?"

"See?" he said triumphantly, pointing his finger at me. "There it is, *now!* It's in your face. You won't let people tell you things. You rush too much. I'm trying to help you and you won't let me." He paused and looked about; the streets were filled with white people. He spoke to me in a low, full tone. "Dick, look, you're black, black, *black*, see? Can't you understand that?"

"Sure. I understand it," I said.

"You don't act a . . . bit like it," he spat.

He then reeled off an account of my actions on every job I had held that summer.

"How did you know that?" I asked.

"White people make it their business to watch niggers," he explained. "And they pass the word around. Now, my boss is a Yankee and he tells me things. You're marked already."

Could I believe him? Was it true? How could I ever learn this strange world of white people?

"Then tell me how must I act?" I asked humbly. "I just want to make enough money to leave."

"Wait and I'll tell you," he said.

At that moment a woman and two men stepped from the jewelry store; I moved to one side to let them pass, my mind intent upon

Grigg's words. Suddenly Griggs reached for my arm and jerked me violently, sending me stumbling three or four feet across the pavement. I whirled.

"What's the matter with you?" I asked.

Griggs glared at me, then laughed.

"I'm teaching you how to get out of white people's way," he said.

I looked at the people who had come out of the store; yes, they were *white*, but I had not noticed it.

"Do you see what I mean?" he asked. "White people want you out of their way." He pronounced the words slowly so that they would sink into my mind.

"I know what you mean," I breathed.

"Dick, I'm treating you like a brother," he said. "You act around white people as if you didn't know that they were white. And they *see* it."

". . . I can't be a slave," I said hopelessly.

"But you've got to eat," he said.

"Yes, I got to eat."

"Then start acting like it," he hammered at me, pounding his fist in his palm. "When you're in front of white people, *think* before you act, *think* before you speak. Your way of doing things is all right among *our* people, but not for *white* people. They won't stand for it."

PROBLEM 7

The Problems of Negro Leadership

From 1890 to the time of World War I, the position of the Negro in the South had deteriorated steadily. During that quarter of a century Southern Negroes had been almost completely deprived of political, economic, and social equality.

Eight Southern states had so restricted the Negro's franchise that his right to vote had virtually been lost. The systems of tenancy, sharecropping, and crop liens in agriculture had given him only crushing poverty. Jim Crow laws had set up effective social, education, and employment barriers between whites and Negroes. In addition, between 1890 and 1900, more than 1200 persons were victims of lynching, and by far the greater number among them were Southern Negroes.

The problem facing Negro leadership was clear: how to narrow the gap between what was preached in a democracy and what was practiced; how to obtain for the Negro the first-class citizenship that was due him as an American.

Among Negro leaders the debate over how to solve these problems waxed vigorously. A few men advocated the use of physical violence to force concessions from the whites. Another small minority urged Negroes to return to Africa or to establish a separate Negro state. The great majority, however, suggested that Negroes use peaceful and democratic means to change undesirable conditions.

Although most Negro leaders agreed that solutions must come gradually, there was little agreement over the best methods to use in solving their problems. Should Negroes fight for civil rights, specifically the right to vote, on the theory that economic and social rights would follow in order? Should Negroes become skilled workers, hoping that if they became indispensable to the prosperity of a region, political and social concessions would have to be given to them? Was academic education more desirable than learning a craft or trade? Should Negroes postpone striving for social equality until they gained political and economic rights? And what did "social equality" mean?

Negro leadership at the turn of the century was divided over what course to follow. The most heated controversy raged between advocates of the gradualist economic approach of Booker T. Washington, with its emphasis on accommodation, and the gradualist political approach of W. E. Burghardt Du Bois, with its emphasis on protest. These two positions remain as guides for many Negroes and Negro organizations today, including the National Association for the Advancement of Colored People and the Urban League. "Sit-in" demonstrations, bus boycotts, the encouragement of vocational education, and stepped-up campaigns to register Negro voters all represent aspects of the positions taken by Washington and Du Bois.

Two selections in Problem 7 are drawn from the writings of Booker T. Washington, the major spokesman for the gradualist economic position. A third is from a book by W. E. Burghardt Du Bois, the chief advocate of political action. In reading the selections, consider the following questions:

1   Upon what points do Washington and Du Bois agree? Where do they disagree? Are there any examples of exaggeration in these accounts?

2   Compare the backgrounds of Washington and Du Bois. What clues do they offer which help account for their views?

3   At two points in the readings, Booker T. Washington uses the phrase "just now." Is this phrase important in making an evaluation of Washington? Explain.

4   Which of the two approaches promised more immediate gains for the Negro?

I

THE ECONOMIC APPROACH

Booker Taliaferro Washington was born in 1856, and spent his boyhood as a slave on a Virginia plantation. After emancipation, his family moved to a small town near Charleston, West Virginia, where work was available in the nearby salt and coal mines. He taught himself to read and write, studying at night and occasionally attending a local school for a few hours in the morning. With a desire to further his education, Washington walked 500 miles in 1872 to enroll at Hampton Institute, a Negro college which had been established by Northern philanthropists.

Washington spent three years at Hampton, learning the trade of a brick-mason and working as a janitor for the institution. After graduation, he taught school in West Virginia for a few years.

In 1881 General Samuel Armstrong, founder of Hampton, recommended Washington for the position of head of a new Negro school, established by Southern philanthropists in Alabama. Thus, Tuskegee Institute was born. During its first year, forty students were enrolled, and their classroom was not more than a "dilapidated shanty." Thirty-four years later, at the time of Washington's death in 1915, Tuskegee had grown to include more than a hundred buildings. It also had 2000 acres of land, an endowment of nearly $2,000,000, and an annual budget of $290,000.

As a result of Washington's work at Tuskegee, his influence reached far beyond the area of education. Presidents of the United States asked his advice when appointing Negroes to federal offices, and in election years his endorsement of the Republican party influenced many Negro voters. Washington supported Negro business enterprises and in 1900 organized the National Negro Business League. He also helped form the Urban League in 1911.

In an address given before a predominantly white audience at the Cotton States' Exposition in Atlanta, Georgia, in 1895, Washington set forth some of his ideas. A few excerpts from his address follow.   □ Booker T. Washington. *Up from Slavery*. New York: Doubleday, Page and Co., 1901, pp. 218–224 passim.

Ignorant and inexperienced, it is not strange that in the first years of our new life we [the Negro freedmen] began at the top instead of at the bottom; that a seat in Congress or the state legislature was more sought than real estate or industrial skill; that the political convention of stump speaking had more attractions than starting a dairy farm or truck garden. . . .

. . . No race can prosper till it learns that there is as much dignity in tilling a field as in writing a poem. It is at the bottom of life we must begin, and not at the top. . . .

. . . you [Southern whites] can be sure in the future, as in the past, that you and your families will be surrounded by the most patient, faithful, law-abiding, and unresentful people that the world has seen. As we have proved our loyalty to you in the past, in nursing your children, watching by the sick-bed of your mothers and fathers, and often following them with tear-dimmed eyes to their graves, so in the future, in our humble way, we shall stand by you with a devotion that no foreigner can approach, ready to lay down our lives, if need be, in defence of yours, interlacing our industrial, commercial, civil, and religious life with yours in a way that shall make the interests of both races one. . . .

The wisest among my race understand that the agitation of questions of social equality is the extremest folly, and that progress in the enjoyment of all the privileges that will come to us must be the result of severe and constant struggle rather than of artificial forcing. No race that has anything to contribute to the market of the world is long in any degree ostracized. It is important and right that all privileges of the law be ours, but it is vastly more important that we be prepared for the exercises of these privileges. The opportunity to earn a dollar in a factory just now is worth infinitely more than the opportunity to spend a dollar in an opera-house.

Washington felt that economic improvement had priority over other concerns and that education should prepare the Negro for this all-important goal. It was natural for Washington to stress vocational education. But what of the Negro's civil rights? Should the Negro participate in politics? Washington's views on education and political activity are set forth in the following selections. □ Booker T. Washington. *The Future of the American Negro*. Boston: Small, Maynard and Company, 1900, pp. 48–51, 131–132, 151–153, 155 passim.

In too large a measure the Negro race began its development at the wrong end . . . [with too much emphasis on academic education]. . . .

In order to emphasise the matter more fully, I repeat, at least eighty per cent of the coloured people in the South are found in the rural districts, and they are dependent on agriculture in some form for their support. Notwithstanding . . . . , very little has been attempted by State or philanthropy in the way of educating the race in this one industry upon which its very existence depends. Boys have been taken from the farms and educated in law, theology, Hebrew and Greek,—educated in everything else except the very subject that they should know most about. . . . It would have seemed that, since self-support, industrial independence, is the first condition for lifting up any race, that education in theoretical and practical agriculture, horticulture, dairying, and stock-raising, should have occupied the first place in our system.

. . . How often has my heart been made to sink as I have gone through the South and into the homes of people, and found women who could converse intelligently on Grecian history, who had studied geometry, could analyse the most complex sentences, and yet could not analyse the poorly cooked and still more poorly served corn bread and fat meat that they and their families were eating three times a day! . . .

In my mind there is no doubt but that we made a mistake at the beginning of our freedom of putting the emphasis on the wrong end. Politics and the holding of office were too largely emphasised, almost to the exclusion of every other interest.

I believe the past and present teach but one lesson,—to the Negro's friends and to the Negro himself,—that there is but one way out, that there is but one hope of solution; and that is for the Negro in every part of America to resolve from henceforth that he will throw aside every non-essential and cling only to essential,—that his pillar of fire by night and pillar of cloud by day shall be property, economy, education, and Christian character. To us just now these are the wheat, all else the chaff. The individual or race that owns the property, pays the taxes, possesses the intelligence and substantial character, is the one which is going to exercise the greatest control in government, whether he lives in the North or whether he lives in the South. . . .

As to such outbreaks as have recently occurred in North Carolina and South Carolina, the remedy will not be reached by the Southern white man merely depriving the Negro of his rights and privileges. . . . I favour the giving up of nothing that is guaranteed to us by the Constitution of the United States, or that is fundamental to our citizenship. While I hold to these views as strongly as any one, I differ with some as to the method of securing the permanent and peaceful enjoyment of all the privileges guaranteed to us by our fundamental law.

In finding a remedy, we must recognise the world-wide fact that the Negro must be led to see and feel that he must make every effort possible, in every way possible, to secure the friendship, the confidence, the co-operation of his white neighbour in the South. To do this, it is not necessary for the Negro to become a truckler or a trimmer. The Southern white man has no respect for a Negro who does not act from principle. In some way the Southern white man must be led to see that it is to his interest to turn his attention more and more to the making of laws that will, in the truest sense, elevate the Negro. . . .

The object-lesson of a thousand Negroes in every county in the South who own neat and comfortable homes, possessing skill, industry, and thrift, with money in the bank, and are large tax-payers co-operating with the white men in the South in every manly way for the development of their own communities and counties, will go a long way, in a few years, toward changing the present status of the Negro as a citizen, as well as the attitude of the whites toward the blacks. . . .

Many have had the thought that industrial training was meant to make the Negro work, much as he worked during the days of slavery. This is far from my idea of it. If this training has any value for the Negro, as it has for the white man, it consists in teaching the Negro how rather not to work, but how to make the forces of nature—air, water, horse power, steam, and electric power—work for him, how to lift labour up out of toil and drudgery into that which is dignified and beautiful.

II

THE POLITICAL APPROACH

W. E. Burghardt Du Bois, editor, author, and veteran campaigner for Negro equality, was born in a small western Massachusetts village in 1868 of mixed Negro, Dutch, and French Protestant ancestry. His youth was spent in an area where he felt little of the sting of discrimination and segregation. As a student at Fisk University in Tennessee, however, Du Bois experienced the full force of Jim Crow, and it had a deep effect upon his thinking. After graduation, Du Bois entered graduate school at Harvard University where in 1895 he became the first Negro to receive the Doctor of Philosophy degree. From 1896 to 1910 he was Professor of Economics and History at Atlanta University and sponsored a series of important studies on the condition of the Negro. Before 1900 Du Bois had been quite sympathetic to the aspirations and goals of Booker T.

Washington. As the years passed, however, he could not accept such a submissive attitude.

In criticizing Washington's policies he became identified as an opponent of Washington and a leader of those who advocated a liberal instead of a vocational education, the restoration and protection of the Negro's right to vote, the repeal of Jim Crow legislation, and a halt to lynching. Du Bois helped to found the National Association for the Advancement of Colored People and was for twenty years the editor of its major publication, *The Crisis*. He became a member of the Communist party in the United States in 1961, and in 1963 was made a citizen of Ghana. He died on August 27, 1963, the day before the Negro Civil Rights March on Washington. ☐ Abridged from *The Souls of Black Folk* by W. E. B. Du Bois. Copyright 1903, by A. C. McClurg & Co.

Easily the most striking thing in the history of the American Negro since 1876 is the ascendancy of Mr. Booker T. Washington. It began at the time when war memories and ideals were rapidly passing; a day of astonishing commercial development was dawning; a sense of doubt and hesitation overtook the freedmen's sons,—then it was that his leading began. Mr. Washington came, with a simple definite programme, . . . His programme of industrial education, conciliation of the South, and submission and silence as to civil and political rights, was not wholly original; the Free Negroes from 1830 up to war-time [1860] had striven to build industrial schools, and the American Missionary Association had from the first taught various trades; and Price [a Free Negro leader] and others had sought a way of honorable alliance with the best of the Southerners. But Mr. Washington first indissolubly linked these things; he put enthusiasm, unlimited energy, and perfect faith into this programme, and changed it from a by-path into a veritable Way of Life. And the tale of the methods by which he did this is a fascinating study of human life. . . .

Mr. Washington represents in Negro thought the old attitude of adjustment and submission; . . . This is an age of unusual economic development, . . . an age when the more advanced races are coming in closer contact with the less developed races, and the race-feeling is therefore intensified; and Mr. Washington's programme practically accepts the alleged inferiority of the Negro races. Again, in our own land, the reaction from the sentiment of war time has given impetus to race-prejudice against Negroes, and Mr. Washington withdraws many of the high demands of Negroes as men and American citizens. . . .

. . . Mr. Washington distinctly asks that black people give up, at least for the present, three things,—

First, political power,

Second, insistence on civil rights,

Third, higher education of Negro youth,—
and concentrate all their energies on industrial education, the accumulation of wealth, and the conciliation of the South. This policy has been courageously and insistently advocated for over fifteen years [about 1885-1900], and has been triumphant for perhaps ten years. As a result of this tender of the palm-branch, what has been the return? In these years there have occurred:

1. The disfranchisement of the Negro.

2. The legal creation of a distinct status of civil inferiority for the Negro.

3. The steady withdrawal of aid from institutions for the higher training of the Negro.

These movements are not, to be sure, direct results of Mr. Washington's teachings; but his propaganda has, without a shadow of doubt, helped their speedier accomplishment. The question then comes: Is it possible, and probable, that nine millions of men can make effective progress in economic lines if they are deprived of political rights, made a servile caste, and allowed only the most meagre chance for developing their exceptional men? If history and reason give any distinct answer to these questions, it is an emphatic *No*. And Mr. Washington thus faces the triple paradox of his career:

1. He is striving nobly to make Negro artisans business men and property-owners; but it is utterly impossible, under modern competitive methods, for workingmen and property-owners to defend their rights and exist without the right of suffrage.

2. He insists on thrift and self-respect, but at the same time counsels a silent submission to civic inferiority such as is bound to sap the manhood of any race in the long run.

3. He advocates common-school and industrial training, and depreciates institutions of higher learning; but neither the Negro common-schools, nor Tuskegee itself, could remain open a day were it not for teachers trained in Negro colleges, or trained by their graduates.

This triple paradox in Mr. Washington's position is the object of criticism by two classes of colored Americans. One class is spiritually descended from Toussaint the Savior, through Gabriel, Vesey, and Turner, and they represent the attitude of revolt and revenge; . . .

The other class of Negroes who cannot agree with Mr. Washington has hitherto said little aloud. They deprecate the sight of scattered counsels, of internal disagreement; and especially they dislike making their just criticism of a useful and earnest man an excuse for a general discharge of venom from small-minded opponents. Nevertheless, the questions involved are so fundamental and serious that it is difficult to see how men like the Grimkes, Kelly Miller, J. W. E. Bowen [the opponents of Washington], and other representatives of this group, can much longer be silent. Such men feel in conscience bound to ask of this nation three things:

1. The right to vote.
2. Civic equality.
3. The education of youth according to ability.

. . . They do not expect that the free right to vote, to enjoy civic rights, and to be educated, will come in a moment; they do not expect to see the bias and prejudices of years disappear at the blast of a trumpet; but they are absolutely certain that the way for a people to gain their reasonable rights is not by voluntarily throwing them away and insisting that they do not want them; that the way for a people to gain respect is not by continually belittling and ridiculing themselves; that, on the contrary, Negroes must insist continually, in season and out of season, that voting is necessary to modern manhood, that color discrimination is barbarism, and that black boys need education as well as white boys. . . .

The black men of America have a duty to perform, a duty stern and delicate, — a forward movement to oppose a part of the work of their greatest leader. So far as Mr. Washington preaches Thrift, Patience, and Industrial Training for the masses, we must hold up his hands and strive with him, rejoicing in his honors and glorying in the strength of this Joshua called of God and of man to lead the headless host. But so far as Mr. Washington apologizes for injustice, North or South, does not rightly value the privilege and duty of voting, belittles the emasculating effects of caste distinctions, and opposes the higher training and ambition of our brighter minds, — so far as he, the South, or the Nation, does this, — we must unceasingly and firmly oppose them. By every civilized and peaceful method we must strive for the rights which the world accords to men, clinging unwaveringly to those great words . . . : "We hold these truths to be self-evident: That all men are created equal; that they are endowed by their Creator with certain unalienable rights; that among these are life, liberty, and the pursuit of happiness."

PROBLEM 8

Origins of the NAACP

Stirred by a race riot, a group of Negroes and whites founded the National Association for the Advancement of Colored People (NAACP) in 1910. The race riot had occurred in 1908 in Springfield, Illinois, and had made shocking headlines across the country. The stories of two Negroes lynched and four whites murdered in the capital of Illinois, a Northern city and the former home of Abraham Lincoln, gave evidence that the South did not have a monopoly on race prejudice.

In an article published in *The Independent*, William English Walling, a journalist and eyewitness of the riot, urged a revival of the nineteenth-century abolitionist spirit of William Lloyd Garrison and John Brown. His plea was answered by Mary Ovington, a white social worker, who invited Walling and others to meet in New York to discuss ways to improve the status of the American Negro. The group decided to hold a national conference, and on May 30, 1909, white and Negro men and women met in New York. They included Oswald Garrison Villard, Mary White Ovington, William Monroe Trotter, Ida Wells Barnett, W. E. Burghardt Du Bois, and others.

Four years earlier, in 1905, Du Bois had been one of the leaders of the Niagara Movement, an organization that demanded an immediate end to disfranchisement, Jim Crow, discrimination in all its forms, and lynching. In a period when Washington's conservative views were popular among Negroes and white, the Niagara group was considered radical. Some members of the Niagara Movement attended the 1909 conference, and because the platform drawn up there was similar in some degree to their own demands, many of the Niagara group joined the new organization. Du Bois became its only Negro officer, and the editor of its publication, *The Crisis*. The Niagara Movement died out after a few years, due partially to the opposition of Booker T. Washington's followers.

Booker T. Washington had been invited to the 1909 conference, but he did not attend. The views of Du Bois and Washington continued to generate controversy within the Negro community over goals and methods to gain their objectives. In reading the selections for Problem 8, consider these questions:

1　With what parts of the first selection would Washington agree? With what parts would he disagree? What sentences and phrases were direct attacks on Washington's leadership?

2　What were the main problems faced by the NAACP in its early years?

3　What is Dr. August Meier's evaluation of Washington? If Washington carried on "underground" work similar to the NAACP, why did he not join the NAACP?

4　Has your opinion of Washington changed since you first read the selections from his biography in Problem 7?

5　Why did Washington's philosophy lose favor following his death in 1915, while Du Bois and the NAACP gained favor?

I

THE NIAGARA MOVEMENT

In its beginning months the Niagara Movement had a membership of fifty-four men, representing eighteen states of the Union. Du Bois was its general secretary, and the Reverend J. M. Waldron of Washington its treasurer. Other officers were state and committee secretaries. Du Bois explains the purposes of the movement in the following excerpt.　□ *The Voice of the Negro*. Atlanta: September 1905, pp. 619–621.

Why this organization is needed. The first exclamation of any one hearing of this new movement will naturally be: "Another!" Why, we may legitimately be asked, should men attempt another organization after the failures of the past? We answer soberly but earnestly, "For that very reason." Failure to organize Negro-Americans for specific objects in the past makes it all the more imperative that we should keep trying until we succeed. . . .

What the Niagara Movement proposes to do. What now are the principles upon which the membership of the Niagara Movement are agreed? As set forth briefly in the constitution, they are as follows:

(a) Freedom of speech and criticism.

(b) An unfettered and unsubsidized press.

(c) Manhood suffrage.

(d) The abolition of all caste distinctions based simply on race and color.

(e) The recognition of the principle of human brotherhood as a practical present creed.

(f) The recognition of the highest and best training as the monopoly of no class or race.

(g) A belief in the dignity of labor.

(h) United effort to realize these ideals under wise and courageous leadership.

All these things we believe are of great and instant importance; there has been a determined effort in this country to stop the free expression of opinion among black men; money has been and is being distributed in considerable sums to influence the attitude of certain Negro papers; the principles of democratic government *are* losing ground, and caste distinctions are growing in all directions. Human brotherhood is spoken of today with a smile and a sneer; effort is being made to curtail the educational opportunities of the colored children; and while much is said about money-making, not enough is said about efficient, self-sacrificing toil of head and hand. Are not all these things worth striving for? *The Niagara Movement* proposes to gain these ends. All this is very well, answers the objector, but the ideals are impossible of realization. We can never gain our freedom in this land. To which we reply: We certainly cannot unless we try. If we expect to gain our rights by nerveless acquiescence in wrong, then we expect to do what no other nation ever did. What must we do then? We must complain. Yes, plain, blunt complaint, ceaseless agitation, unfailing exposure of dishonesty and wrong—this is the ancient, unerring way to liberty, and we must follow it. I know the ears of the American people have become very sensitive to Negro complaints of late and profess to dislike whining. Let that worry none. No nation on earth ever complained and whined so much as this nation has, and we propose to follow the example. Next we propose to work. These are the things that we as black men must try to do.

To press the matter of stopping the curtailment of our political rights.

To urge Negroes to vote intelligently and effectively.

To push the matter of civil rights.

To organize business co-operation.

To build school houses and increase the interest in education.

To open up new avenues of employment and strengthen our hold on the old.

To distribute tracts and information in regard to the laws of health.

To bring Negroes and labor unions into mutual understanding.

To study Negro history. . . .

To attack crime among us by all civilized agencies. In fact to do all in our power by word or deed to increase the efficiency of our race, the enjoyment of its manhood, rights and . . . duties. . . .

This is a large program. It cannot be realized in a short time. But something can be done and we are going to do something.

II

EARLY YEARS OF THE NAACP

On the centenary of Abraham Lincoln's birth, February 12, 1909, Mary White Ovington, William English Walling, and Henry Moskovitz published *The Call*. It was a statement written by Oswald Garrison Villard, grandson of William Lloyd Garrison, recounting injustices suffered by Negroes and calling for a conference in their behalf. After its publication, arrangements for the conference proceeded, and scientists and educators gladly accepted invitations to speak at the meetings.   ☐ From *The Walls Came Tumbling Down* by Mary White Ovington. Copyright, 1946, by Harcourt Brace Jovanovich, Inc. and reprinted with their permission. Pp. 105–107, 108–110, 111–113, 115–117.

But if choosing speakers went ahead smoothly, the work of those who were to bring in names of men and women to form a permanent committee was far from simple. Certain names occurred at once—

Moorfield Storey and Albert E. Pillsbury of Boston, Bishop Alexander Walters of New York, and Charles E. Bentley of Chicago. We could form a satisfactory working committee, but would we be able to raise money unless it included Booker T. Washington?

I have spoken before of Washington's power. Villard, a newspaper owner, appreciated this more than some of the others. If you wanted to raise money in New York for anything relating to the Negro, you must have Washington's endorsement. This was a bald statement, but we had to have money to put over our program. We would need money for publicity, for an office, for legal work. We were a group primarily of white people who felt that while the Negro would aid in the Committee's work (we were then called the National Negro Committee) the whites, who were largely responsible for conditions and who controlled the bulk of the nation's wealth, ought to finance the movement. But how to get such support without Washington's endorsement?

Well, we anti-Washingtonians won out . . . .

. . . Not until the following year, when we again met in New York, did we become the National Association for the Advancement of Colored People, incorporated under the law by the State of New York. . . .

The average age of the five incorporators, Du Bois, Villard, Walter E. Sachs, for a time treasurer, John Haynes Holmes, and myself, was thirty-five. I like to remember this because it is rarely until old age that men are recognized, that their portraits are painted, or their statues placed in parks. . . .

Our first practical job was a case concerned with an arrest at Asbury Park, New Jersey, of a Negro charged with murder. There was no evidence against him, but he was black and had been near the scene of the crime. He was put through the third degree before we learned of the case. Our lawyer went at once to Asbury Park and after some days secured his release. A similar case occurred later at Lakewood, New Jersey. This time we moved more quickly, found that there was no evidence, and freed the man. Imagine our satisfaction when we learned that we had been "rather expected," that there was an organization in New York that was looking into these Negro arrests. Our fame had crossed the North River!

The expense of our work fell upon a few people. Oswald Garrison Villard gave us room-rent in the *Evening Post* building and many hours a week of his time. He won friends for us, and gave us much publicity in his paper. . . . We struggled under the expense of irregularly paid counsel until in 1913 Arthur B. Spingarn and Charles H. Studin took over our legal work, carrying it on in their office. "And do you know," Richetta Randolph, our office secretary said once to me, "no matter how many times I call Mr. Spingarn up, and sometimes I call him three or four times in one day, he is never annoyed, never gives me the feeling that I should not have troubled him." This arrangement continued until 1936 when Charles H. Houston, a Harvard graduate and a man of legal experience, became our Special Counsel. He carried on the work of our office and was able to be of definite help. . . . All the time we were building up a list of lawyers, white and colored, in various parts of the United States, who could be called upon when needed. . . .

What were we doing besides legal work in these formative years before World War I had put new demands upon us? What direction did our "Advancement" program take?

It did not enter the field of social service and employment. Most fortunately, about six months after we began, the Urban League was formed. George Haynes, sociologist from Fisk University, came into our office one morning with plans to form a national organization in the fields of employment and of philanthropy. . . . Some of us gasped at having so large a field of "advancement" taken out of our program, but nothing could have been more fortunate. We could not have raised money for "philanthropy" as successfully as an organization with a less militant program, and securing employment is a business in itself. So the two national organizations divided the field, working together from time to time as action demanded.

The newspapers usually showed the Negro as a criminal. It made, they thought, interesting reading. We, then, would show the criminality of the white; we would publicize lynching, interpret the story which, in 1911, appeared in the papers on an average of every six days —the story of a colored man taken out of the custody of the law and lynched.

A map of the United States soon appeared in our office with a pin stuck into every spot where there had been a lynching. The lower part of the map was black with pinheads. Our primer was a post card that had been sent to John Haynes Holmes after he had spoken against lynching in Ethical Cultural Hall. We had tried to get ministers of established position in New York to speak at this meeting but without success. "We must get young men," Villard then declared, "newcomers who at once will write themselves down as opposed to this shame of America." We did get two such men, the Reverend John Haynes Holmes and Rabbi Stephen S. Wise. . . . Our publicity must soon have reached the South, for shortly after the meeting Holmes came to us with a post card which he had received from a town where a lynching occurred. It was a picture post card. In the foreground was the dead Negro, and back of him, and on both sides, were the lynchers, clear-cut photographs that could have been used successfully for identification. The men's confidence that no one would dream of prosecuting them was the most striking thing about the card. We wondered that it had been permitted to go through the United States mail.

We used that post card with accounts of other lynchings as publicity. . . .

Lynching was not the only form of violence that came to our attention. The attempted destruction of homes bought by Negroes in white neighborhoods was becoming frequent, and cities were passing segregation ordinances to prevent such transfer of property. Homes of Negroes who had bought houses in white blocks or nearly white blocks were bombed, dynamited, and occupants were intimidated in many cities. Philadelphia had a case in which a colored woman, buying a home and finding it damaged and her family in danger, demanded and got police protection for six months. Negroes in Baltimore, Kansas City, Louisville, and other cities sent us stories of destruction of property. . . .

When the NAACP brought its test case before the Supreme Court, it was not without some support from real estate operators. The Louisville Segregation Case was a test of the validity of the city's segregation ordinance which the Kentucky Court of Appeals had held valid. When the case came before the Supreme Court of the United States, that court reversed the decision. . . . Moorfield Storey won this, our second case. Our first case, the "Grandfather Clause Case" he also won for us, and his presence before the Supreme Court set the highest standard for our growing organization. The Grandfather Clause of the Oklahoma Constitution was declared unconstitutional in 1915. It was part of an amendment to the Constitution of Oklahoma passed in 1910, and provided that no person should be registered unless he were able to read and write. But should the would-be voter be denied the right because he could not read or write, he still might vote if his lineal ancestor had been eligible prior to

Jan. 1, 1866. This ingenious method of disfranchising Negroes while enfranchising illiterate whites with a slaveholding tradition was declared unconstitutional.

III

AN EVALUATION OF BOOKER T. WASHINGTON

This reading was written especially for this book by August Meier, Associate Professor of History at Morgan State College in Baltimore, Maryland. Dr. Meier has written extensively on the Negro in general and on Booker T. Washington in particular. His recent book, *Negro Thought in America 1880 – 1915* (University of Michigan, 1963), covers the high period of Washington's influence. Quotations by Dr. Meier are taken from the Washington papers and correspondence in the Library of Congress.

Although in his public statements Washington minimized the value of political and civil rights, he secretly worked hard at making a direct attack on disfranchisement and other forms of discrimination. He was responsible for the Negroes appointed to office by Presidents Roosevelt and Taft, and he strongly opposed the trend toward the entire loss of the Negro's political rights in the South. Washington lobbied extensively against a bill intended to disfranchise Georgia Negroes in 1899. And once the Southern states had passed amendments to their constitutions disfranchising Negroes, he secretly financed cases that tested the constitutionality of the Alabama and Louisiana amendments in the federal courts. To assure secrecy while this work was carried on, the correspondence about it was handled by Washington's secretary and a lawyer in New York under assumed names. In addition to his personal contributions, Washington appealed to his friends among white philanthropists for funds to help fight these cases. Thus in 1903 and 1904, as he wrote a friend, he personally "spent at least four thousand dollars in cash, out of . . . [his] own pocket . . . in advancing the rights of the black man." Unfortunately Washington's efforts in this matter were not successful. He also fought a vigorous and what turned out to be a hopeless battle against the Lily-White Republicans of the South who were trying to eliminate Negroes from the party in that section. His correspondence is full of material on the subject. As he wrote to one of his closest associates in this fight in 1905, "What I have attempted in

Louisiana, I have attempted to do in nearly every one of the Southern states, as you and others are in a position to know, and but for my action, feeble as it was, the colored people would have been completely overthrown and the Lily-Whites would have been in complete control in nearly every Southern state."

Washington also engaged in activities against Jim Crow car laws. As early as 1901 a friend of his in Richmond, Virginia, had taken up his suggestion of testing in the courts the Virginia Jim Crow laws. When the Pullman Company decided that, since state laws required separate accommodations, it would exclude Negroes entirely from its sleeping cars, Washington worked with an interested group of Negroes to start legal action against the company. At his request, a close personal friend, who was also a prominent railway official, discussed the matter with the president of Pullman, but the Pullman Company did not alter its decision.

In other areas Washington proved more successful. Two important cases were aimed at excluding Negroes from Southern juries. Washington contributed money and worked very closely with the lawyer responsible until they won the cases in the Supreme Court. Washington was active in certain cases where Negro sharecroppers had been sentenced to the chain gang for violating the terms of their contract, either accidentally or from a lack of knowledge. He became deeply involved in a peonage case. (Peonage is a system whereby individuals are forced into virtual slavery as a result of debts or from a lack of understanding in making contracts.) It was a long, drawn-out fight, and as Washington informed his friends, ". . . some of us here have been working at this case for over two years." They secured the free services of "some of the best lawyers in Montgomery," and the help of other prominent people in Alabama. The case was fought up to the Supreme Court, where it was ruled that peonage is unconstitutional.

Thus, it is evident that—unknown to the vast majority of his admirers—Washington was actually behind the scenes directing a frontal attack on disfranchisement, segregation, and other kinds of discrimination. Contrary to his conciliatory manner toward the white South and his emphasis upon economic advancement as the chief method of solving the race problem, he was working along the very lines that the Niagara Movement and the NAACP employed openly.

PROBLEM 9

The Chicago Race Riot

World War I was over. The world had been made "safe for democracy." In February 1919, a million New Yorkers lined Fifth Avenue to welcome troops, including the Negro 369th Regiment, returning from France. A few days afterward, Negro soldiers paraded through downtown Chicago to the cheers of thousands. Five months later, twenty-three Negroes and fifteen whites lay dead on the streets of this same city as a result of racial violence. In the last six months of 1919, twenty-five race riots occurred in cities all over the country.

Negroes and whites together had proudly shed their blood for America; now fellow Americans were drawing one another's blood. What had happened? The answers are difficult to uncover. Consideration must be given to the mood of America in the months following the armistice that ended the war. Rumors of Communist subversion swept the country. One Indiana jury deliberated two minutes before acquitting a citizen who had shot and killed a man for yelling, "To hell with the United States!" Time bombs had been mailed to prominent Americans. A rash of strikes paralyzed the nation. The racial conflicts must be judged within this setting of anxiety and fear.

Another factor to consider is the impact of the war upon the Negro. Thousands who had fought for democracy in the trenches of France expected to live freely in America. A half-million Negroes had moved from the South to the North where economic, social, political, and educational opportunities beckoned to them. With a spirit of confidence, the American Negro looked forward to a new position in society—a position unfettered by Jim Crow practices.

However, Jim Crow practices and attitudes were not affected by the war. Northern and Southern racial prejudices did not change. Negroes often met violence when they tried to assert their rights. Mounting tension, friction, and hate form the dynamite of race riots. Only a spark—a crime or the rumor of one—is required to ignite it.

The following readings are selected from the report of the Chicago Commission on Race Relations, which was formed shortly after the 1919 riot to study race problems in Chicago. The first reading describes the riot; the others deal with trends and attitudes.

1   What was the immediate cause of the Chicago race riot? Why do you think rioting continued?

2   How reliable are the newspaper accounts given in Reading II? How might newspapers have played a constructive role?

3   How was the Thomas family unprepared for a new life in Chicago? How might the inexperience of people like the Thomases and the Joneses antagonize whites?

4   What economic motives for prejudice against Negroes do you find in readings IV and V?

5   What are the chief attitudes described in Reading VI? Do you feel that the evidence offered in their support is valid?

I

THE RIOT

☐ Chicago Commission on Race Relations. The Negro in Chicago, pp. 596-598. Reprinted by permission of the University of Chicago Press. Copyright 1922 by the University of Chicago.

Sunday afternoon, July 27, 1919, hundreds of white and Negro bathers crowded the lake-front beaches at Twenty-sixth and Twenty-ninth streets. This is the eastern boundary of the thickest Negro residence area. At Twenty-sixth Street Negroes were in great majority; at Twenty-ninth Street there were more whites. An imaginary line in the water separating the two beaches had been generally observed by the two races. . . . This line served virtually as a challenge to either side to cross it. Four Negroes who attempted to enter the water from the "white" side were driven away by the whites. They returned with more Negroes, and there followed a series of attacks with stones. . . .

Eugene Williams, a Negro boy of seventeen, entered the water from the side used by Negroes and drifted across the line supported by a railroad tie. He was observed by the crowd on the beach and promptly became a target for stones. He suddenly released the tie, went down and was drowned. Guilt was immediately placed on Stauber, a young white man, by Negro witnesses who declared that he threw the fatal stone. (The coroner's jury found that Williams had drowned from fear of stonethrowing which kept him from the shore.)

White and Negro men dived for the boy without result. Negroes demanded that the policeman present arrest Stauber. He refused; and at this crucial moment arrested a Negro on a white man's complaint. Negroes then attacked the officer. These two facts, the drowning and the refusal of the policeman to arrest Stauber, together marked the beginning of the riot.

Two hours after the drowning, a Negro, James Crawford, fired into a group of officers summoned by the policeman at the beach and was killed by a Negro policeman. Reports and rumors circulated rapidly, and new crowds began to gather. Five white men were injured in clashes near the beach. As darkness came Negroes in white districts to the west suffered severely. Between 9:00 P.M. and 3:00 A.M. twenty-seven Negroes were beaten, seven stabbed, and four shot. Monday morning was quiet, and Negroes went to work as usual.

Returning from work in the afternoon many Negroes were attacked by white ruffians. Street-car routes, especially at transfer points, were the centers of lawlessness. Trolleys were pulled from the wires, and Negro passengers were dragged into the street, beaten, stabbed, and shot. The police were powerless to cope with these numerous assaults. During Monday, four Negro men and one white assailant were killed, and thirty Negroes were severely beaten in street-car clashes. Four white men were killed, six stabbed, five shot, and nine severely beaten. It was rumored that the white occupants of the Angelus Building at Thirty-fifth Street and Wabash Avenue had shot a Negro. Negroes gathered about the building. The white tenants sought police protection, and one hundred policemen, mounted and on foot, responded. In a clash with the mob the police killed four Negroes and injured many. . . .

On Tuesday, July 29, Negro men en route on foot to their jobs through hostile territory were killed. White soldiers and sailors in uniform, aided by civilians, raided the "Loop" business section, killing two Negroes and beating and robbing several others. Negroes living among white neighbors . . . were driven from their homes, their household goods were stolen, and their houses were burned or wrecked. On the West Side an Italian mob, excited by a false rumor that an Italian girl had been shot by a Negro, killed Joseph Lovings, a Negro.

Wednesday night at 10:30 Mayor Thompson yielded to pressure and asked the help of the three regiments of militia which had been stationed in nearby armories during the most severe rioting, awaiting the call. They immediately took up positions throughout the South Side. A rainfall Wednesday night and Thursday kept many people in their homes, and by Friday the rioting had abated. On Saturday incendiary fires burned forty-nine houses in the immigrant neighborhood west of the Stock Yards. Nine hundred and forty-eight people, mostly Lithuanians, were made homeless, and the property loss was about $250,000. Responsibility for the fires was never fixed.

The total casualties of this reign of terror were thirty-eight deaths—fifteen white, twenty-three Negro—and 537 people injured.

II

RUMORS DURING THE RIOT

The tension between Negroes and whites during the riot was heightened by the wide circulation of rumors among members of both races. These rumors spread like wildfire, inciting further mob violence. The newspaper accounts in this reading show how the same rumor was changed to fit white or colored readership. ☐ The Negro in Chicago, pp. 30, 31.

Chief among the anger-provoking rumors were tales of injury done to women of the race circulating the rumor. The similarity of the stories and their persistence shows extraordinary credulity on the part of the public. For the most horrible of these rumors, telling of the brutal killing of a woman and baby (sometimes the story is told of a Negro woman, sometimes of a white) there was no foundation in fact. The story was circulated not only by the newspapers of both races, but was current always in the crowds on the streets. Here is the story as told in the white press:

"There is an account of 'two desperate revolver battles fought by the police with colored men alleged to have killed two white women and a white child.'

"It is reported that policemen saw two Negroes knock down a woman and child and kick them. The Negroes ran before the police could reach them." (*Chicago Tribune*, July 29)

"Two white women, one of them with a baby in her arms, were attacked and wounded by Negro mobs firing on street cars. . . .

"A colored woman with a baby in her arms was reported at the Deering Police Station, according to this item, to have been attacked by a mob of more than 100 white men. When the mob finally fled before the approach of a squad of police both the woman and child were lying on the street beaten to death, 'it is said.'" (*Herald-Examiner*, July 29)

". . . The Negroes, four in number, were arrested . . . this afternoon by the detective. They are believed to be the ones who seriously wounded Mrs. Margaret Kelley, white woman, at 47th and Wentworth. She was shot in the back and may die. The names of those under arrest were not given out." (*Daily News*, July 29) [A police report indicated that the woman, a Mrs. Mary Kelly, was shot in the arm, and not in the back.] . . .

Here is . . . [the same] story as it appeared in the Negro press:

"An unidentified young woman and three-months-old baby were found dead on the street at the intersection of Forty-seventh and Wentworth. She had attempted to board a car there when the mob seized her, beat her, slashed her body to ribbons, and beat the baby's brains out against a telegraph pole. . . . The whole time this was happening several policemen were in the crowd but did not make any attempt to make a rescue until too late." (*Chicago Defender*, August 2)

Concerning all of these stories it may be stated that the coroner had no cases of deaths of women and children brought before him. There was nothing in the police reports or the files of the state's attorney or hospital reports or the reports of Olivet Baptist Church, which would give any foundation for reports of the killing of a woman and child, white or Negro.

III

THE NEGRO MIGRANT IN CHICAGO

During the two years before the Chicago riot, the Negro population of the North was swelled by some 500,000 migrants from the South. The Negro population in Chicago jumped 148.5 per cent during the decade of 1910 to 1920, from 44,103 to 109,594. (The increase of whites in Chicago for the same period was only 21 per cent.) The typical new Negro in Chicago had fled the total segregation of the South to seek the freedom of the North. He did find better working conditions and access to many public facilities formerly denied him, but he also faced a host of problems. Some of these are described in the following studies of two migrant Negro families in Chicago. ☐ The Negro in Chicago, pp. 95-97.

The Thomas family—Mr. Thomas, his wife and two children, a girl nineteen and a boy seventeen, came to Chicago from Seals, Alabama, in the spring of 1917. . . . Mr. and Mrs. Thomas were farmers in the South. On the farm Mrs. Thomas did the work of a man along with her husband. Both are illiterate. The daughter had reached the fourth grade and the boy the fifth grade in school. At home they belonged to a church and various fraternal orders and took part in rural community life.

On their arrival in Chicago they were short of funds. Father and son went to work at the Stock Yards. Although they had good jobs they found their income insufficient; the girl went to work in a laundry, and the mother worked as a laundress through the first winter for $1 a day. She later discovered that she was working for half the regular rate for laundry work. . . .

All the family were timid and self-conscious and for a long time avoided contacts, thus depriving themselves of helpful suggestions. The children became ashamed of the manners of their parents and worked diligently to correct their manner of speech. . . .

The freedom and independence of Negroes in the North have been a constant novelty to them and many times they have been surprised that they were "not noticed enough to be mistreated." They have tried out various amusement places, parks, ice-cream parlors, and theaters near their home on the South Side and have enjoyed them because they were denied these opportunities in their former home. . . .

The Jones family. — Mr. Jones, his wife, a six-year-old son, and a nephew aged twenty-one, came from Texas early in 1919. Although they arrived after the heaviest migration, they experienced the same difficulties as earlier comers.

They searched for weeks for a suitable house. At first they secured one room on the South Side in a rooming-house, where they were obliged to provide gas, coal, linen, bedding, and part of the furniture. After a few weeks they got two rooms for light housekeeping, for $10 a month. . . . [Their neighbors and] the physical condition of the house were intolerable. They then rented a flat on Carroll Avenue in another section. The building was old and run down. The agent for the property, to induce tenants to occupy it, had promised to clean and decorate it, but failed to keep his word. When the Jones family asked the owner to make repairs, he refused flatly and was exceedingly abusive.

Finally Jones located a house on the West Side that was much too large for his family, and the rent too high. They were forced to take lodgers to aid in paying the rent. This was against the desire of Mrs. Jones, who did not like to have strangers in her house. The house has six rooms and bath and is in a state of dilapidation. Mr. Jones has been forced to cover the holes in the floor with tin to keep out the rats. The plumbing is bad. During the winter there is no running water, and the agent for the building refuses to clean more than three rooms or to furnish screens or storm doors or to pay for any plumbing. In the back yard under the house is an accumulation of ashes, tin cans, and garbage left by a long series of previous tenants. . . . Jones made a complaint about insanitary conditions to the Health Department, and the house was inspected, but so far nothing has been done. . . .

They [the Jones family] had been told that no discrimination was practiced against Negroes in Chicago; that they could go where they pleased without the embarrassment or hindrance because of their color. Accordingly, when they first came to Chicago, they went into drug-stores and restaurants. They were refused service in numbers of restaurants and at the refreshment counters in some drugstores. The family has begun the re-establishment of its community life, having joined a West Side Baptist church and taking an active interest in local organizations, particularly the Wendell Phillips Social Settlement. The greatest satisfaction of the Joneses comes from the "escape from Jim Crow conditions and segregation" and the securing of improved conditions of work, although there is no difference in the wages.

IV

CONFLICTS OVER HOUSING

Racial tension was perhaps greatest in white areas adjacent to Negro sections of Chicago. Fearful that property values would decline sharply, white home owners organized themselves to keep Negroes out of their neighborhoods. The activities of one South Side home owners' organization are reported in the following excerpt. ☐ *The Negro in Chicago,* pp. 118–119.

It does not appear that the residents . . . rose spontaneously to oppose the coming in of Negroes. If this had been the case, the first Negroes moving into the district in 1917 would have felt the opposition. The sudden interest in race occupancy was based upon the alleged depreciation of property by Negroes. With this emphasized, it was not difficult to rally opposition to Negroes as a definite menace. The real estate men gave the alarm, alleging a shrinkage in property values. The effort through the Hyde Park and Kenwood Association was intended to stop the influx and thereby the depreciation. Meetings were held, a newspaper was published, and literature was distributed. Racial antagonism was strong in the speeches at these meetings and in the newspapers. The meeting which probably marked the first focusing of attention on the Kenwood and Hyde Park districts was held May 5, 1919, when the sentiment was expressed that Negro invasion of the district was the worst calamity that had struck the city since the Great Fire. A prominent white real estate man said: "Property owners should be notified to stand together block by block and prevent such invasion."

Distinctly hostile sentiments were expressed before audiences that came expecting to hear how their property might be saved from "almost certain destruction." . . .

"The depreciation of our property in this district has been two hundred and fifty millions since the invasion. If someone told you that there was to be an invasion that would injure your homes to that extent, wouldn't you rise up as one man and one woman, and say . . . 'They shall not pass'?" . . .

"Why I remember fifteen or twenty years ago that the district down here at Wabash Avenue and Calumet was one of the most beautiful and highest-class neighborhoods of this great city. Go down there today and see the ramshackle broken-down and tumble-down district. That is the result of the new menace that is threatening this great Hyde Park district. And then tell me whether there are or not enough red-blooded, patriotic, loyal, courageous citizens of Hyde Park to save this glorious district from the menace which has brought so much pain and so much disaster to the district to the south of us."

The attempt to keep the Negro out was not limited to speeches at meetings. Prior to the riot, there were twelve bombings of Negro residences in Chicago. Many more occurred afterwards. Typical bombings are described in this reading. □ *The Negro in Chicago*, pp. 124–125, 128–129.

Bombing of the Motley home. — In 1913 S. P. Motley, Negro, and his wife purchased a building at 5230 Maryland Avenue through a white agent, and on March 15, 1913, the family moved in. For four years they lived there without molestation save the silent resentment of neighbors and open objection to the presence of Negro children in the streets. On July 1, 1917, without warning or threat, a bomb was exploded in the vestibule of the house, and the front of the building was blown away. The damage amounted to $1,000. Police arrived . . . ten minutes after the explosion. No clews were found and no arrests were made. The original owner of the building was bitterly opposed to Negroes and was a member of an organization which was seeking to keep Negroes out of the district.

Some time after this incident it was rumored that Motley was planning to purchase the building adjacent. At 4:00 A.M. June 4, 1919, a dynamite bomb was exploded under the front of the house adjacent and tore up its stone front. . . . No clews were found and no arrests were made. . . .

Bombing of the Harrison home. — Mrs. Gertrude Harrison, Negro, living alone with her children, contracted to buy a house at 4708 Grand Boulevard. In March, 1919, she moved in. She immediately received word that she had committed a grave error. She and her children were constantly subjected to the insulting remarks both of her immediate neighbors and passers-by.

On May 16, 1919, a Negro janitor informed her that neighbors were planning to bomb her house. She called up the Forty-eighth Street police station and told of the threatened danger. The officer answering the telephone characterized her report as "idle talk" and promised to send a man to investigate. The regular patrolman came in and promised to "keep an eye on the property," but there were ten blocks in his beat. A special guard was secured and paid by Mrs. Harrison when it was learned that one would not be furnished by the police.

The following night, May 17, her house was bombed while the patrolman was "punching his box" two blocks away and the special watchman was at the rear. A detail of police was then provided both at the front and rear. The following night a bomb was thrown on the roof of the house from the window of a vacant flat in the adjoining apartment house. The flat from which the bomb was thrown had been unlocked to admit the bombers and locked again. The police failed to question either the persons living in the apartment or those leaving it immediately after the explosion. . . . No arrests were made.

V

NEGRO STRIKEBREAKERS

A strike offered the unemployed Negro a way to earn a few days' wages and a chance for permanent employment. It offered revenge for the Negro who had been denied membership in the striking union. It also generated a hatred for the Negro race among white workers. □ *The Negro in Chicago*, pp. 430–431.

Some of the most conspicuous cases coming to the attention of the Commission in which Negroes have taken the place of white strikers or have remained at work during strikes are the following:

The Stock Yards strike of 1904 lasted from July 4 to the middle of September. The general superintendent of one of the plants in the

Yards, appearing before the Commission, said: "The strike was called at 12:00 o'clock. Every employee practically that we had went out: Within two or three days we had any number of colored employees return to work. . . . I'd say Negroes helped us to break the strike by coming to work. A number of Negroes that we understand belonged to the union did not remain out more than two or three days. Practically all the Negroes came back before the strike was called off."

The strike in the Corn Products Refining Company plant at Argo, where, in the summer of 1919, before the strike, 300 Negroes were employed, during the strike 900, and when it was over about 500.

The steel strike of 1919. Representatives of several of the iron and steel plants stated that Negroes had helped to break this strike. The *Inter-Church World Movement Report on the Steel Strike of 1919* (p. 177) lists the "successful use of strike-breakers, principally Negroes, by the steel companies" as the second cause of the failure of the steel strike. "'Niggers did it' was a not uncommon remark among company officials." . . .

During a strike, feeling runs high and the word "strike breaker" or "scab" carries with it a decided stigma among the strikers. White workers ordinarily do not try to understand why the Negro acts as he does. They do not reason that the Negro is often loyal to the employer because he feels that the employer, sometimes at considerable risk, has opened to him industrial opportunities which, translated into wages, mean better living conditions for himself and his family. . . . White workers feel that Negroes who serve as strike breakers are helping to earn for their race the stigma of being a "scab" race. This is especially serious in the case of Negroes, because color identification makes it easy to focus hatred for the "scab."

VI

"NIGGERS ARE DIFFERENT FROM WHITES"

To find out some of the basic causes of the 1919 riot, the Chicago Commission on Race Relations questioned a number of white persons about their feelings toward Negroes.   ☐ *The Negro in Chicago,* pp. 438–439, 452–453.

The chief of these [attitudes] is that the mind of the Negro is distinctly inferior to that of the white race; . . . that the mind of the Negro cannot be improved above a given level or beyond a given age; that his education should be adapted to his capacities, that is, he should mainly be taught to use his hands. Thus a teacher in one of the elementary schools of Chicago finds that "colored children are restive and incapable of abstract thought; they must be constantly fed with novel interests and given things to do with their hands." Accordingly they are given handicraft instead of arithmetic, and singing instead of grammar.

In seeking the opinion of white trades unionists on the admission of Negroes to unions in Chicago, the Commission encountered in perhaps the harshest form the conviction that Negroes were inherently unable to perform tasks that white men did as a matter of course. A member of the Brotherhood of Locomotive Engineers felt that no Negro had, or could ever acquire, intelligence enough to run an engine. Employers frequently expressed the belief that Negroes are incapable of performing tasks which require sustained mental application. . . .

A teacher in a Chicago public school said: "I believe . . . that when a Negro boy grows a mustache his brain stops working."

A teacher in Moseley School said: "The great physical development of the colored person takes away from the mental, while with the whites the reverse is true. . . ."

A physician . . . said: "The increasing amount generally of sex immorality is being contributed to by mixing Negroes and whites in schools and parks."

A teacher . . . said: "The colored people are coming from the South all the time, for political purposes. It's propaganda for the colored man to sit down by the white woman, and not to double up to make room for the whites. Their papers tell them to do it. I was the only white person in an empty car one day and a colored man came in and took the seat beside me." . . .

A resident in . . . [an integrated neighborhood] said: "A colored family lives next door north of me, and you'll be surprised when I tell you that I haven't been able to open my bedroom window on that side to air that room for three years. I couldn't think of unlocking the windows because their window is so near somebody could easily step across into this house. It's awful to have to live in such fear of your life."

When asked if she considered her neighbors so dangerous as that, she said: "Well, no, the woman seems pretty nice. I see her out in the back yard occasionally and bid her the time of day out of charity. You can't help but pity them, so I am charitable and speak. Where the danger really is, is that you never know who's in their house; they bring such trash to the neighborhood, even if they are good and decent. How do I know what kind of people this woman next door associates with? There's awful-looking people sit on the front porch sometimes. Why, I couldn't sit on my porch on the hottest day because I'd be afraid they would come out any minute. And what white person will sit on a porch next door to a porch with black ones on it? Not me, anyhow, nor you either I hope."

Another resident said: "I have nothing against the black man as a black man. He comes into my place of business (drug-store) and I sell him. Not many come in, as there aren't a lot of colored people around here. But I don't want to live with niggers any more than you or any other white person does. People who say, 'I like the colored people and don't see why others can't get along with them' don't talk practical common sense. Theoretically all this talk is all right, but you get a white man of this sort to come right down and live with a nigger and he won't do it.

"Niggers are different from whites and always will be, and that is why white people don't want them around. But the only thing we can do, it seems to me, is make the best of it and live peaceably with them. The North can never do what the South does—down there it is pure autocracy. I might say like Russia. That might have worked here in the North from the start, but can't be started now, and we wouldn't want such autocracy anyway. They are citizens, and it is up to us to teach them to be good ones. How it can be done I don't know—it will have to come slow, and no one can give a solution offhand. Everybody says, 'We don't want the niggers with us.' Well, here they are, and we can't do anything. Must let them live where they want to and go to school where they want to, and we don't want to force their right away."

PROBLEM 10

The Harlem Renaissance

In the 1920's a group of talented Negroes poured their feelings into prose, poetry, art, music, and drama. Their work constituted the Negro Renaissance, or Harlem Renaissance after New York's famous Negro district where this artistic movement was centered. During the Harlem Renaissance, white America "discovered" its talented brown citizens and Negro artists rode the crest of popularity. African art became the rage; whites journeyed to Harlem nightclubs to hear jazz; major publishing companies brought out books about Negroes written by Negroes; plays about Negroes, starring Negroes, appeared on Broadway; Negro and white scholars began serious studies of Negro life. It was truly a renaissance.

The roots of the Harlem Renaissance can be found in the literary interest in the Negro that developed before and during World War I. The Harlemites received considerable support from prominent white writers. Equally important are the postwar factors (described in Problem 9) that contributed to a new self-confidence on the part of the Negro. The postwar Negro was proud, defiant, and bitter—proud of his skin color, defiant toward a country that treated him disdainfully, and bitter at the injustices of the whole Jim Crow system. Consider the exclamation of W. E. B. Du Bois: "Make way for Democracy! We saved it for France, and by the Great Jehovah, we will save it in the U.S.A., or know the reason why."

Pride, defiance, and bitterness were present in the work of the Harlem Renaissance artists. Far more important was the quality of their products, for they were skilled craftsmen in expressing the feelings of the new Negro. Many of these writers, however, were not solely interested in race. The standard of artistic quality was just as important to them as to their white counterparts; they wished to be judged as poet, artist, or novelist—not as *Negro* poet, *Negro* artist, or *Negro* novelist.

The career of Langston Hughes, poet and novelist, gives an insight into this artistic movement. Of Negro, Indian, and white ancestry, Hughes was born in Joplin, Missouri, in 1902. His youth was spent moving from one place to another: Kansas, Mexico, Illinois, and finally Cleveland, Ohio. He met Jim Crow life in one part of the country, ghetto life in another. Hughes knew the full meaning of being a Negro in white America. Indeed his experiences gave him a broad view of life itself. At various times, Hughes was a seaman, tutor of English in Mexico, doorman, cook in Paris nightclubs, clerk, and college student. Through all of these experiences, he refined his skill as a poet. He had written his first poem after he was elected "class poet" in his elementary school in Illinois. Apparently, his white classmates thought all Negroes were musical and rhythmic. In this instance, a stereotype was fulfilled.

Central to his literary career was the conviction that a writer should write of what he knows best and Hughes identified with the mass of Negro people. His poems "tried to capture some of the dreams and heartaches that all Negroes know." Hughes had a deep feeling of oneness with his race. Recalling an incident in his youth when he traveled on an old freighter to Africa, he wrote, "My Africa, Motherland of the Negro People! And me a Negro! Africa! The real thing, to be touched and seen not merely read about in a book." And he recalls his disappointment at not being considered a Negro in Africa because he was "brown," not black.

Hughes never accepted the degraded condition of Negroes in America. Indignation at the Southern color line rings out from the pages of his autobiography. Thus, Langston Hughes combined racial pride with artistic skill to create militant literature typical of the

Harlem Renaissance. Indeed, within Hughes was the essence of the Harlem Renaissance.

Two years after the stock market crash of 1929, the Renaissance was no more. Literary interest in the Negro dwindled. But not for Langston Hughes. His stated purpose, "to write seriously and as well as I knew about the Negro people" continued to guide his work.

1   Do you agree with Hughes' criticism of the Negro poet? What is the main point of the essay?

2   What examples of racial pride, defiance, and bitterness can be found in Reading II?

3   Are Reading II and Reading III consistent with the views expressed by Hughes in Reading I?

4   How do the selections reflect the spirit of the Harlem Renaissance? How do they reflect Hughes' background?

I

THE NEGRO ARTIST AND THE RACIAL MOUNTAIN

In this essay, Langston Hughes challenges Negro writers to be proud of their color and the customs of their race. □ "The Negro Artist and the Racial Mountain" by Langston Hughes. Copyright 1926 by Langston Hughes. Reprinted by permission of Harold Ober Associates Incorporated.

One of the most promising of the young Negro poets said to me once, "I want to be a poet—not a Negro poet," meaning, I believe, "I want to write like a white poet"; meaning subconsciously, "I would like to be a white poet"; meaning behind that, "I would like to be white." And I was sorry the young man said that, for no great poet has ever been afraid of being himself. And I doubted then that, with his desire to run away spiritually from his race, this boy would ever be a great poet. But this is the mountain standing in the way of any true Negro art in America—this urge within the race toward whiteness, . . . to be as little Negro and as much American as possible.

But let us look at the immediate background of this young poet. His family is of what I suppose one would call the Negro middle class: people who are by no means rich yet never uncomfortable nor hungry—smug, contented, respectable folk, members of the Baptist church. The father goes to work every morning. He is a chief steward at a large white club. The mother sometimes does fancy sewing or supervises parties for the rich families of the town. The children

go to a mixed school. In the home they read white papers and maga-
zines. And the mother often says "Don't be like niggers" when the
children are bad. A frequent phrase from the father is, "Look how well
a white man does things." And so the word white comes to be un-
consciously a symbol of all the virtues. It holds for the children
beauty, morality, and money. The whisper of "I want to be white"
runs silently through their minds. This young poet's home is, I believe, a fairly typical home of the colored middle class. One sees
immediately how difficult it would be for an artist born in such a home
to interest himself in interpreting the beauty of his own people. He is
never taught to see that beauty. He is taught rather not to see it, or if
he does, to be ashamed of it when it is not according to Caucasian
patterns. . . . A very high mountain indeed for the would-be
racial artist to climb in order to discover himself and his people.

But then there are the low-down folks, the so-called common
element, and they are the majority—may the Lord be praised! The
people who have their nip of gin on Saturday nights and are not too
important to themselves or the community, or too well fed, or too
learned to watch the lazy world go round. They live on Seventh Street
in Washington or State Street in Chicago and they do not particularly
care whether they are like white folks or anybody else. Their joy
runs, bang! into ecstasy. Their religion soars to a shout. Work maybe
a little today, rest a little tomorrow. Play awhile. Sing awhile. O, let's
dance! These common people are not afraid of spirituals, as for a long
time their more intellectual brethren were, and jazz is their child.
They furnish a wealth of colorful, distinctive material for any artist
because they still hold their own individuality in the face of American
standardizations. And perhaps these common people will give to the
world its truly great Negro artist, the one who is not afraid to be himself. Whereas the better-class Negro would tell the artist what to do,
the people at least let him alone when he does appear. And they are
not ashamed of him—if they know he exists at all. And they accept
what beauty is their own without question. . . .

We younger Negro artists who create now intend to express our
individual dark-skinned selves without fear or shame. If white people
are pleased we are glad. If they are not, it doesn't matter. We know we
are beautiful. And ugly too. . . . If colored people are pleased
we are glad. If they are not, their displeasure doesn't matter either.
We build our temples for tomorrow, strong as we know how, and we
stand on top of the mountain, free within ourselves.

II

CONVERSATION

In a Langston Hughes novel, two elderly Negro widows discuss their lives. Aunt Hager is a laundress, and Sister Whiteside sells garden produce. The boy Sandy is Hager's grandson. The rows of dots in this excerpt are not ellipses (unless bracketed) but indicate pauses in the conversation. ☐ From *Not Without Laughter* by Langston Hughes. Copyright 1930, by Alfred A. Knopf, Inc. Reprinted by permission of the publisher. Pp. 20–29.

Hager uncovered a pot that had been simmering on the stove all morning and dished up a great bowlful of black-eyed peas and salt pork. There was biscuit bread left from breakfast. A plate of young onions and a pitcher of lemonade stood on the white oilcloth-covered table. Heads were automatically bowed.

"Lawd, make us thankful for this food. For Christ's sake, amen," said Hager; then the two old women and the child began to eat.

"That's Elvira's boy, ain't it—that yaller-headed young-one was here playin' with Sandy?" Sister Whiteside had her mouth full of onions and beans as she asked the question.

"Shsss! . . . That's her child!" said Hager. "But it ain't Eddie's!" She gave her guest a meaning glance across the table, then lowered her voice, pretending all the while that Sandy's ears were too young to hear. "They say she had that chile 'fore she married Eddie. An' black as Eddie is, you knows an' I knows ain't due to be no golden hair in de family!"

"I knowed there must be something funny," whispered the old sister, screwing up her face. "That's some white man's chile!"

"Sho it is!" agreed Hager. . . . "I knowed it all de time. . . . Have some mo' meat, Whiteside. Help yo'self! We ain't got much, but such as 'tis, you're welcome. . . . Yes, sir, Buster's some white man's chile. . . . Stop reachin' cross de table for bread, Sandy. Where's yo' manners, sir? I declare, chillens do try you sometimes. . . . Pass me de onions."

"Truth, they tries you, yit I gits right lonesome since all ma young ones is gone." Sister Whiteside worked her few good teeth vigorously, took a long swallow of lemonade, and smacked her lips. "Chillen an' grandchillen all in Chicago an' St. Louis an' Wichita, an' nary chick nor child left with me in de house. . . . Pass me de bread, thank yuh. . . . I feels kinder sad an' sorry at times, po'

widder-woman that I is. I has ma garden an' ma hens, but all ma chillens done grown and married. . . . Where's yo' daughter Harriett
at now, Hager? Is she married, too? I ain't seen her lately."

Hager pulled a meat skin through her teeth; then she answered:
"No, chile, she too young to marry yet! Ain't but sixteen, but she's
been workin out this summer, waitin' table at de Stanton County
Country Club. Been in de country three weeks now, since school
closed, but she comes in town on Thursdays, though. It's nigh six
miles from here, so de women-help sleeps there at night. I's glad
she's out there, Sister. Course Harriett's a good girl, but she likes
to be frisky — wants to run de streets 'tendin' parties an' dances, an' I
can't do much with her no mo', though I hates to say it."

"But she's a songster, Hager! An' I hears she's sho one smart
chile, besides. They say she's up with them white folks when it comes
to books. An' de high school where she's goin' ain't easy. . . . All
ma young ones quit 'fore they got through with it — wouldn't go —
ruther have a good time runnin' to Kansas City an' galavantin' round."

"De Lawd knows it's a hard job, keepin' colored chillens in
school, Sister Whiteside, a mighty hard job. De niggers don't help
'em, an' de white folks don't care if they stay or not. An' when they
gets along sixteen an' seventeen, they wants this, an' they wants that,
an' t'other — an' when you ain't got it to give to 'em, they quits school
an' goes to work. . . . Harriett says she ain't goin' back next fall.
I feels right hurt over it, but she 'clares she ain't goin' back to school.
Says there ain't no use in learnin' books fo' nothin' but to work in
white folks' kitchens when she's graduated."

"Do she, Hager? I's sho sorry! I's gwine to talk to that gal. Get
Reverend Berry to talk to her, too. . . . You's struggled to bring
up yo' chillens, an' all we Christians in de church ought to help you! I
gwine see Reverend Berry, see can't he 'suade her to stay in school."
The old woman reached for the onions. "But you ain't never raised no
boys, though, has you, Hager?"

"No, I ain't. My two boy-chillens both died 'fore they was ten.
Just these three girls — Tempy, an' Annjee, an' Harriett — that's all I
got. An' this here grandchile, Sandy. . . . Take yo' hands off that
meat, sir! You had 'nough!"

"Lawd, you's been lucky! I done raised seven grandchillen 'sides
eight o' ma own. An' they don't thank me. No, sir! Go off and kick up
they heels an' git married an' don't thank me a bit! Don't even write,
some of 'em. . . . Waitin' fo' me to die, I reckon, so's they can

squabble over de little house I owns an' ma garden." The old visitor pushed back her chair. "Huh! Yo' dinner was sho good! . . . Waitin' fo' me to die."

"Unhuh! . . . That's de way with 'em, Sister Whiteside. Chillens don't care—but I reckon we old ones can't kick much. They's got to get off fo' themselves. It's natural, that's what 'tis. Now, my Tempy, she's married and doin' well. Got a fine house, an' her husband's a mail-clerk in de civil service makin' good money. They don't 'sociate no mo' with none but de hightoned colored folks, like Dr. Mitchell, an' Mis' Ada Walls, an' Madam C. Frances Smith. Course Tempy don't come to see me much 'cause I still earns ma livin' with ma arms in de tub. But Annjee run in their house out o' the storm last night an' she say Tempy's just bought a new pianer, an' de house looks fine. . . . I's glad fo' de chile."

"Sho, sho you is, Sister Williams, you's a good mother an' I knows you's glad. But I hears from Reverend Berry that Tempy's done withdrawed from our church an' joined de Episcopals!"

"That's right! She is. Last time I seed Tempy, she told me she couldn't stand de Baptist no mo'—too many low niggers belonging, she say, so she's gonna join Father Hill's church, where de best people go. . . . I told her I didn't think much o' joinin' a church so far away from God that they didn't want nothin' but yaller niggers for members, an' so full o' forms an' fashions that a good Christian couldn't shout—but she went on an' joined. It's de stylish temple, that's why, so I ain't said no mo'. Tempy's goin' on thirty-five now, she's ma oldest chile, an' I reckon she knows how she wants to act.

"Yes, I reckon she do. . . . But there ain't no church like de Baptist, praise God! Is there, Sister? If you ain't been dipped in that water an' half drowned, you ain't saved. Tempy don't know like we do. No, sir, she don't know!"

There was no fruit or dessert, and the soiled plates were not removed from the table for a long time, for the two old women, talking about their children, had forgotten the dishes. [. . .]

"Now, ma girl, Maggie," said Sister Whiteside; "de man she married done got to be a big lawyer in St. Louis. He's in de politics there, an' Maggie's got a fine job herself—social servin', they calls it. But I don't hear from her once a year. An' she don't send me a dime. Ma boys looks out for me, though, sometimes, round Christmas. There's Lucius, what runs on de railroad, an' then Andrew, what rides de horses, an' John, in Omaha, sends me a little change now an' then

—all but Charlie, an' he never was thoughtful bout his mother. He ain't never sent me nothin'."

"Well, you sho is lucky," said Hager; "'cause they ain't no money comes in this house, Christmas nor no other time, less'n me an' Annjee brings it here. Jimboy ain't no good, an' what Harriett makes goes for clothes and parties an' powderin'-rags. Course, I takes some from her every week, but I gives it right back for her school things. An' I ain't taken nothin' from her these three weeks she's been workin' at de club. She say she's savin' her money herself. She's past sixteen now, so I lets her have it. . . . Po' little thing! . . . She does need to look purty." Hager's voice softened and her dark old face was half abashed, kind and smiling. "You know, last month I bought her a gold watch—surprise fo' her birthday, de kind you hangs on a little pin on yo' waist. Lawd knows, I couldn't 'ford it—took all de money from three week's o'washin', but I knowed she's been wantin' a watch. An' this front room—I moved ma bed out last year an' bought that new rug at de second-hand store an' them lace curtains so's she could have a nice place to entertain her comp'ny. . . . But de chile goes with such a kinder wild crowd o' young folks, Sister Whiteside! It worries me! The boys, they cusses, an' the girls, they paints, an' some of 'em live in de Bottoms. I been tried to get her out of it right along, but seems like I can't. That's why I's glad she's in de country fo' de summer an' comes in but only once a week, an' then she's home with me. It's too far to come in town at night, she say, so she gets her rest now, goin' to bed early an' all, with de country air round her. I hopes she calms down from runnin' round when she comes back here to stay in de fall. . . . She's a good chile. She don't lie to me 'bout where she goes, nor nothin' like that, but she's just wild, that's all, just wild."

"Is she a Christian, Sister Williams?"

"No, she ain't. I's sorry to say it of a chile o' mine, but she ain't. She's been on de moaner's bench time after time, Sunday mawnins' an' prayer-meetin' evenin's, but she never would rise. I prays for her."

"Well, when she takes Jesus, she'll see de light! That's what de matter with her, Sister Williams, she ain't felt Him yit. Make her go to church when she comes back here. . . . I reckon you heard 'bout when de big revival's due to come off this year, ain't you?"

"No, I ain't, not yet."

"Great colored tent-meetin' with de Battle-Ax of de Lawd, Reverend Braswell preachin'! Yes, sir! Gwine start August eighteenth in de Hickory Woods yonder by de edge o' town."

"Good news," cried Hager. "Mo' sinners than enough's in need o' savin'. I's gwine to take Sandy an' get him started right with de Lawd. An' if that onery Jimboy's back here, I gwine make him go, too, an' look Jesus in de face. Annjee an' me's saved, chile! . . . You Sandy, bring us some drinkin'-water from de pump." Aunt Hager rapped on the window with her knuckles to the boy playing outside! "An' stop wrastlin' with that gal."

Sandy rose triumphant from the prone body of black little Willie-Mae, lying squalling on the cinderpath near the back gate. "She started it," he yelled, running towards the pump. The girl began a reply, but at that moment a rickety wagon drawn by a white mule and driven by a grey-haired, leather-colored old man came rattling down the alley.

"Hy, there, Hager!" called the old Negro, tightening his reins on the mule, which immediately began to eat corn-tops over the back fence. "How you been treatin' yo'self?"

"Right tolable," cried Hager, for she and Sister Whiteside had both emerged from the kitchen and were approaching the driver. "How you doin', Brother Logan?"

"Why, if here ain't Sis' Whiteside, too!" said the old beau, sitting up straight on his wagon-seat and showing a row of ivory teeth in a wide grin. "I's doin' purty well for a po' widower what ain't got nobody to bake his bread. Doin' purty well. Hee! Hee! None o' you all ain't sorry for me, is you? How de storm treat you, Hager? . . . Says it carried off yo' porch? . . . That's certainly too bad! Well, it did some o' these white folks worse'n that. I got 'nough work to do to last me de next fo' weeks, cleanin' up yards an' haulin' off trash, me an' dis mule here. . . . How's yo' chillen, Sis' Williams?"

"Oh, they all right, thank yuh. Annjee's still at Mis' Rice's [where she is a cook], an' Harriett's in de country at de club."

"Is she?" said Brother Logan. "I seed her in town night 'fore last down on Pearl Street 'bout ten o'clock."

"You ain't seed Harriett no night 'fore last," disputed Hager vigorously. "She don't come in town 'ceptin' Thursday afternoons, an' that's tomorrow."

"Sister, I ain't blind," said the old man, hurt that his truth should be doubted. "I—seen—Harriett Williams on Pearl Street . . . with Maudel Smothers an' two boys 'bout ten o'clock day before yes-tidy night! An' they was gwine to de Waiters' Ball, 'cause I asked Maudel where they was gwine, an' she say so. Then I says to Harriett: 'Does yo' mammy know you's out this late?' an' she laughed an' say: 'Oh, that's all right!' . . . Don't tell me I ain't seen Harriett, Hager."

"Well, Lawd help!" Aunt Hager cried, her mouth open. "You done seed my chile in town an' she ain't come anear home! Stayed all night at Maudel's, I reckon. . . . I tells her 'bout runnin' with that gal from de Bottoms. That's what makes her lie to me—tellin' me she don't come in town o' nights. Maudel's folks don't keep no kind o' house, and mens goes there, an' they sells licker, an' they gambles an' fights. . . . Is you sho that's right, Brother Logan, ma chile done been in town an' ain't come home?"

"It ain't wrong!" said old man Logan, cracking his long whip on the white mule's haunches. "Gittiyap! You old jinny!" [. . .]

"Um-uh!" said Sister Whiteside to Hager as the two toil-worn old women walked toward the house. "That's de way they does you!" The peddler gathered up her things. "I better be movin', 'cause I got these greens to sell yit, an' it's gittin' 'long towards evenin'. . . . That's de way chillens does you, Sister Williams! I knows! That's de way they does!"

III

SONG TO A NEGRO WASH-WOMAN

Oh, wash-woman,
Arms elbow-deep in white suds,
Soul washed clean,
Clothes washed clean,
I have many songs to sing you
Could I but find the words.

Was it four o'clock or six o'clock on a winter afternoon,
    I saw you wringing out the last shirt in Miss White
Lady's kitchen? Was it four o'clock or six o'clock
    I don't remember.

But I know, at seven one spring morning you were on
Vermont Street with a bundle in your arms going to
wash clothes.

And I know I've seen you in the New York subway in
the late afternoon coming home from washing
clothes.

Yes, I know you, wash-woman.

I know how you send your children to school, and
high-school, and even college.
I know how you work to help your man when times are
hard.
I know how you build your house up from the washtub
and call it home.
And how you raise your churches from white suds for
the service of the Holy God.

I've seen you singing, wash-woman. Out in the backyard
garden under the apple trees, singing, hanging white
clothes on long lines in the sunshine.
And I've seen you in church on Sunday morning singing,
praising your Jesus because some day you're going to
sit on the right hand side of the Son of God and
forget you ever were a wash-woman.
And the aching back and the bundles of clothes will be
unremembered then.

Yes, I've seen you singing.

So for you,
O singing wash-woman,
For you, singing little brown woman,
Singing strong black woman,
Singing tall yellow woman,
Arms deep in white suds,
Soul washed clean,
Clothes washed clean,
For you I have
Many songs to sing
Could I but find the words.

PROBLEM 11

Class Structure in the Negro Community

In which social class — upper, middle, or lower — would the following person be included?

Occupation: lawyer
Education: Harvard graduate
Income: $20,000 a year

Residence: large home in a
    fashionable part of town
Religion: Episcopalian

Usually a lawyer with these qualifications would rank in the upper half of the middle class. But if the lawyer were a Negro, would his social standing be affected? The answer to this question lies in the fact that America does not have a single class structure. There is a Negro class system and a white class system separated by a wall of color. The Negro system exists on a lower level than the white system, that is, Negroes are generally looked down upon regardless of their social background.

Many similarities exist in the two class systems. Occupation, income, and education — to a great extent — determine social class for both Negroes and whites. In general, a Negro doctor or lawyer and his white counterpart rank high in their respective social class systems. White or Negro unskilled laborers rank low in class. Another similarity is the mobility within each class structure. Consider the humble beginnings of prominent whites and Negroes, such as baseball stars Joe DiMaggio and Jackie Robinson or public figures Arthur Goldberg and Ralph Bunche.

However, the two class structures are not precisely parallel. A comparison shows the Negro upper and middle classes to be proportionately smaller than the same white classes, and the Negro lower class to be proportionately larger than the white lower class. Racial discrimination largely accounts for this disproportion. A Jim Crow education and limited job opportunities help perpetuate poverty. Even with higher education, the Negro encounters discrimination. The average income of white college graduates is greater than that of black college graduates.

Within the Negro class structure, shade of skin often affects social standing. Upper-class Negroes generally have lighter skin than lower-class Negroes. This distinction has its roots in history. For 350 years American Negroes have been told in a thousand different ways of the advantages of a light skin. Economic opportunity, freedom from discrimination, and the exercise of one's rights go hand in hand with being white. Under such conditions some Negroes come to hate their color. This may explain the use of skin whiteners and hair straighteners or a desire to marry a lighter skinned mate. Some Negroes whose coloring is light have chosen to cross the color line and "pass" as white. But with rising militancy and emphasis on black pride, a reversal of values has occurred. The favorable use of the term "black" is evidence of the changed attitude toward dark skin color. Some blacks, especially young people, take pride in their African heritage by wearing the "Afro" or "bush" hair style, which features unstraightened hair, or African-style clothing, such as the loose-fitting dashikis and colorful bubas.

The Negro social class structure is not static. After World War II, higher incomes, better education, and a wider range of occupational choice generated changes within the Negro community. The readings for Problem 11 analyze these changes and explore the characteristics of the various Negro classes. In reading, consider these questions:

1 What are the main characteristics of each Negro class? Which of these characteristics would hold true for white classes? In what ways have white American values influenced Negro America?

2 How does religion reflect social class among Negroes? How does the evidence in Reading II relate to the views on religion expressed by Langston Hughes in his essay and novel (Problem 10)?

3   According to Reading III, what is the range of attitudes of middle-class Negroes toward low-income Negroes?

I

DEFINING THE CLASSES

An American Dilemma, written in the early 1940's by Swedish sociologist Gunnar Myrdal, is considered an outstanding work on the American Negro. The following selection is taken from a condensation of Myrdal's two-volume book. ☐ From *The Negro in America*, the condensed version of Gunnar Myrdal's *An American Dilemma* by Arnold Rose. Copyright 1944, 1948 by Harper & Row, Publishers, Inc. By permission of the publishers. Pp. 227-230.

The Negro lower class contains the large majority of Negroes. They are the unskilled or semiskilled laborers and domestic workers of the cities in the South and in the North; and the agricultural wage laborers, tenants, and household servants in the Southern rural districts.   .   .   .   Lower-class Negroes generally have little education. The older generation is often illiterate or practically so. Books, periodicals, and newspapers, social movements and ideas (except for the Negro problem), play insignificant roles in their lives.

The class is Southern in origin and character. Even in the Northern cities the lower class of Negroes is largely made up of recent migrants from the South and of their children.   .   .   .

To a section of the lower class belong the chronic relief cases, the habitual criminals, prostitutes, gamblers, and vagabonds. In the upper levels of the lower class there are many persons who have definite ambitions to better their own, or at least their children's, status. These people will take care not to let their insurance lapse; they will have permanent affiliation with churches and lodges; they will try to keep their children in school.

At the other end of the social scale is the small Negro upper class. In rural districts the ownership and successful management of a sizable farm may give a person upper-class status. All over the country training for a profession or the carrying on of a substantial business, particularly in the field of banking or insurance, but also in contracting, real estate, and personal service, is the basis for an upper-class position.   .   .   .   Generally, in the relative absence of wealth, higher education is becoming almost an essential to an upper-class position. Light skin color and other white features also are associated with upper-class status, especially among Negro women. This basis of distinction grew up in slavery times, when the white master's slave children had a better chance of gaining freedom and getting an education and when house servants—often selected because of their "nice" appearance—had more privileges than the field slaves.

Often family background is stressed in the upper class. The family is organized upon the paternalistic principle, legal marriage is an accepted form, and illegitimacy and desertion are not condoned. Children are shielded as far as possible both from influences of the lower-class Negroes and from humiliating experiences of the caste system. They are ordinarily given a higher education and professional training. As Negroes are commonly believed to be loud, ignorant, dirty, and lax in sexual and all other morals, good manners and respectability become nearly an obsession in the Negro upper class. . . .

. . . The Negro upper class is characterized by many of the traits that are in complete contrast to those of the masses of Negroes in the lower class. Their social ambition is to keep up this distinction. In private they are often the severest critics of the Negro masses.

The Negro middle class is usually assumed to be larger than the upper class but smaller than the lower class. Members of the middle class have achieved a small but, in comparison with the lower class, less insecure occupational position. However, they are characterized even more by a striving toward a better economic position. They have typically had primary education and, not infrequently, secondary education, but few have been to college except the school teachers. Education has a high ranking in their scale of values, and they want to give their children this means of fuller cultural emancipation. They also look down on the lower-class Negroes and attempt to be respectable. Thrift, independence, honesty, and industriousness are included in their standards. In the middle class it becomes a proud boast never to have been in trouble with the law. Family life is rather stabilized. . . .

The foregoing picture of the Negro class structure is, like most other descriptions, static. Actually, the Negro class structure is dynamic: not only is there movement between the classes and changes within each of the classes, but also the entire class system is moving upward.

II

CLASS ATTITUDES TOWARD RELIGION

In studying the Chicago Negro community in the early 1940's, St. Clair Drake and Horace Cayton found that religious attitudes usually reflected the various class divisions. ☐ From *Black Metropolis* by St. Clair Drake and Horace Cayton. Copyright 1945 by Harcourt Brace Jovanovich, Inc., and reprinted with their permission. Pp. 537, 538, 539, 611, 670, 672, 673.

There are some entire denominations as well as a few individual churches that have the reputation of being upper-class. Traditionally the Episcopal Church has symbolized upper-class standards, with its high proportion of upper-class members. Congregational and Presbyterian churches have enjoyed the same reputation. Owing to the small size of the upper class, however, no congregation has a majority of upper-class members, though there are some in which such persons exercise dominance, and in which mobile individuals from the other classes look to the upper-class members to "set the pace."

One woman of moderately high social status thinks that the Congregational Church is "based on a 'solid' group of people, for if a person in that church were not socially educated, he would not enjoy it." . . . Other Congregationalists say, "Our church is simple, dignified and modern"; "People of the upper stratum come here." etc. . . .

The pastors of the upper-class churches are all college-trained men of wide experience. Their sermons are usually scholarly in form and devoid of the cruder emotional tricks common in many other churches. . . .

In general, it seems that though formal membership in some church is expected of older persons who wish to maintain status within the upper class, active participation is not required of either men or women. There is, however, a "church-centered" segment of the upper class which participates actively in the affairs of the churches mentioned. These persons not only have wide contacts with prominent Negroes, but their church relations often bring them into contact with prominent white persons. One Negro businessman boasted that he was on the Episcopal Diocesan Council with several of the most outstanding white bankers and businessmen in America. Upper-class members tend to monopolize the handling of funds and the general planning in the churches with which they are associated, and often express themselves quite frankly as believing that it "pays" to be affiliated with a church. Membership in very low-status churches would be definitely taboo, however. . . .

. . . [In "Bronzeville," Chicago's Negro district, there are about] 500 churches, at least 300 of these being located in definitely lower-class neighborhoods. The evening hours of Bronzeville's lower-class areas are noisy with the cacophony of both hymns and blues, gospel songs and "low-down" music. It is obvious that some people in Bronzeville take their pleasure by "making a joyful noise unto the Lord." . . .

When a person in Bronzeville says that he is "sanctified" or that he attends a Spiritualist church or one of the "cults," he is immediately marked down as "low-status." We have referred . . . to the fact that the members and preachers of these churches are well aware that they are "looked down on." If a man says he's an Episcopalian or a Congregationalist, Bronzeville thinks of him as "dicty" or a "strainer" or "striver" [upper-class Negro]. But if he says he's Baptist or Methodist or Catholic he can't be "placed" until he tells what specific congregation he belongs to. Some entire denominations are "class-typed," but among the larger denominations there are "class-typed" congregations *within* the group. There are, for instance, one or two Methodist and Baptist churches that have the reputation of "catering to high-toned people," and there are scores of churches that are of very low status—usually store-fronts.

If we examine what the opponents of store-fronts have to say about them, we get some clues as to what makes a church low-status. A rather comfortably situated Catholic housewife comments on her religious preferences as follows:

"I like good music, but I don't like the songs that these gospel choirs in the store-fronts sing—these jazz tunes. I think it is heathen-like to jazz hymns. Another thing about these store-fronts is all these funny 'isms'—like giving a person a rose that's been blessed with the idea of bringing good luck. Some people actually believe these fool things." . . .

A Congregational pastor, however, was somewhat more moderate in his appraisal:

"There is no doubt that some 'jack-leg' preachers [those without formal religious training] are charlatans, but some aren't. A good many of them are ministering to folks that I just couldn't minister to. . . .

The folks a 'jack-leg' preacher has to handle are in such a socio-economic and educational position that they just wouldn't understand me. They need an outlet for their embittered emotions. Their lives are pretty much disorganized. The 'jack-leg' preacher fills a need. He may be ignorant and utterly uninformed in the respects that we think a preacher should be trained, but he has a useful role."

Even while justifying the existence of the store-front, however, this minister reveals the class gulf between his upper-middle-class congregation and lower-class church people. . . .

Most of Bronzeville's middle-class church people belong to what one student has called the "mixed-type" congregation, one that incorporates both lower-class and middle-class features in its ritual and its pattern of organization. Most of the very large congregations and many of the medium-sized churches try to hold together in one congregation the people who like "rousements" and "shouting," as well as those who prefer a more restrained service. The pastor of a large church must cater to those who like the "old-time religion" as well as to the more modern members. Such ministers become adept at keeping the allegiance of both groups.

To satisfy middle-class members, an astute pastor of a mixed-type church will present a "prepared message" with moral and ethical exhortation and intelligent allusions to current affairs; but he will also allow his lower-class members to shout a little. Such shouting is usually rigidly controlled, however, so that it does not dominate the service. Since most of the pastors of the larger churches are seminary-trained men with a middle-class orientation, and some are university men with advanced degrees, they do not want to be classed as "ignorant" or "uncultured," nor do they wish to alienate professional and businessmen, or younger people who reject the "old-time religion."

So a skillful pastor will rigorously control the emotional display by changing the tone of his sermon at strategic points to stimulate shouting, shutting it off before it gets out of hand. Thus, one very astute performer shouts his audience violently and then suddenly stops, with a remark such as the following:

"My, I forgot where I was this morning. I musta thought I was still down between the plow-handles and not here in a Chicago pulpit. Lemme get back to this paper (manuscript). I forgot I had these educated folks in here. But I'm not ashamed of my Jesus!" (There will be a chorus of *"Amens"* and some laughter, and the shouting will be over for a while.)

III

THE MODERN MIDDLE CLASS: ATTITUDES TOWARD RACE

Since 1960, there has been a phenomenal rise in the number of middle-class black families. In this newspaper article, several Negroes discuss the gap that exists between middle-class and poor Negroes. Their opinions reveal the tension generated by this gap. ☐ Abridgement of 1362 words from "The Modern Middle Class: Attitudes Toward Race" from *The Los Angeles Sentinel* (January 18, 1968). Reprinted by permission of Los Angeles Sentinel.

. . . Who belongs to the New Negro Middle Class? Some may quibble with our definition but . . . here's how we portray the group:

Economically, they earn more than $10,000 and less than $50,000 a year, whether on the labors of one or two members of a family unit. They reside primarily in homes valued between $25,000 and $75,000, in residential areas, whether predominately Negro or white, in which there are strong school systems supported by aggressive parental groups. As a class, they are exceedingly well educated, most having college degrees, professional degrees, specialized training, or some part thereof.

They're doctors, lawyers, engineers, educators, accountants, salesmen, government employees, specialists in various endeavors of business enterprises, entertainers, artists, technicians, and consultants, among many other things.

Their children are exposed to and offered the "extras" in life. Swimming lessons, dancing classes, little league, music lessons, horseback riding, vacations, plays, their own individual rooms, and the best of medical and dental care, not to mention expensive and stylish clothing.

This then, is the class of which we are speaking.

One hot, humid day last summer, at the height of the Detroit riots, an attractive, stylishly dressed Negro woman, approaching 40, was waiting at a downtown Los Angeles intersection for her husband to pick her up from a day of shopping. As she waited, she read with disgust the blaring headlines on an afternoon newspaper which trumpeted the bloody deeds taking place in the Michigan city.

"It just makes you sick, doesn't it?" a Caucasian woman standing near her said.

"Yes, yes it certainly does," the woman answered without really seeing the woman standing next to her. "And to think that they're doing it to my city, my hometown! I was born and grew up in those areas they're burning. I still have friends and relatives who live back there. I just hope they're all right."

The Caucasian woman looked with genuine sympathy at the woman and almost without thinking said:

"You must feel doubly bad since those are your people causing trouble for your own people."

For the first time, the Negro woman looked at the Caucasian woman straight on and replied with contempt:

"I remember the words of a World War II general when someone says that to me. They are of my color but not of my kind." . . .

. . . Is this a typical middle-class attitude?

"Why shouldn't it be?" asked a nice-looking young Negro professional man when I posed the question to him . . . . "Just because a man happens to belong to the same racial group I do, does this mean I must necessarily have to apologize for or be identified with every wrong he does?"

"You believe, then, to riot is a wrong?" I asked him.

"Of course I do. I have fallen out of bed with the civil rights movement since it's taken a turn towards violence. Violence only creates hatred, hardened attitudes, stiffening positions, and, in the end, only total destruction."

A few days later, while talking to an avowed and committed Black Nationalist, I asked him the same question. His answer:

"Of course it's a Negro Middle Class attitude. I would say 'Black' but those folks with money and good jobs have forgotten what it's like to be black. They consciously tried to forget what it's like. They are now whiter than white in their attitudes and outlooks. I won't disgrace the word by calling them 'Black.' They are just what they should be called: 'Negroes,' living in a false world with a degrading name."

"How can you be sure that those in this class have forgotten, to use your word, what it's like to be black?" I asked.

"I have but to look no further than the pages of the newspaper you write for to prove my point. All of the space is devoted to social and entertainment coverage. There are other things in life, brother, more important to the black man than what rich man's daughter got married and who's appearing at the local gin mill that's probably owned by the white beast to begin with. Until the black man in America is free, every black publication in the country should eliminate all but essential stories."

"What do you mean by 'essential'?" I queried.

"Those stories that deal only with the black man on the street throwing off the yoke of the white oppressors," was the answer.

On a cool, clear evening in early October, I was sitting in a Westwood bar having a drink with a very successful Negro sales executive, a man who has risen up the ladder of success to the point where he and his family are enjoying, very well, the fruits of his hard labors. I asked him:

"Do you think that the Negro Middle Class has a detached attitude towards the struggling, less affluent members of the race?"

He thought a moment before answering:

"People ask me this question a lot, both Negroes and Caucasians. I must be honest and say . . . that it depends on the individual. Some people, regardless of their ethnic background or economic status, are just more self-involved than others and these are the people who could care less than a darn about what problems and conflicts others are being faced with, even though they themselves have at one time or another been faced with the same circumstances."

"Be more specific," I suggested. "What about you?"

"I care about the problems of those less fortunate Negroes and I demonstrate this caring by belonging to two separate organizations which, in varied ways, are attempting to give assistance in the ways we believe are most beneficial. However, I am not going to be intimidated as some Black Militants and others have attempted to intimidate more affluent Negroes. I am not going to be made to feel guilty or something less than human simply because I have worked hard to attain a certain amount of financial and social status in our society. Sure, I was lucky and had some great helping hands but there was a lot of hard work, privation and personal dedication also."

A couple of days later . . . I had lunch with a young Negro engineer employed by one of the big missile firms. I asked him the same question:

"Sure I'm detached from those who revel in what is really a pseudo-African culture with the naturals and all that. Sure I'm detached from those who go around preaching separatism, black nationalism, and hatred based simply on skin coloring. And, maybe I'm detached from those who live in an all-Negro social structure . . . . I'm detached because that's not the life I live and that's not the life

I want for myself and my family."

"Don't you believe that you have a responsibility to the race?" I asked.

"The only responsibility I have," he shot back, "is to my wife, my children, and to myself. Other than that, if I pay my taxes and obey the laws, I have nobody else to answer to or for."

One warm July afternoon last summer, a couple of days before the Fourth of July celebration, I was sitting near the pool at the home of a well-fixed Caucasian friend and was introduced to a bright young Negro professional man. During the conversation, the man told me that he was looking for a "large place" in which to live. I suggested looking in a rolling, rural area which seemed to fit the description of the type property he was seeking.

"I wouldn't move way out there and be away from my people," the man said, almost angrily. "I would feel guilty if I moved my family away from my soul sisters and brothers. They would lose not only their touch with reality but with our heritage."

PROBLEM 12

Black Voting in the South

"Sure, I reckon it's all right for a nigger to vote if he wants to and it don't harm nothing, but what if they all begun to vote here! We'd be swamped. You put *yourself* in *our* place and you'll see why we got to keep *them* in *their* place."

This statement, made by a white Tennessean from a county with a large Negro population, sums up segregationist Southern opinion on voting. Disfranchisement is one of the white supremacists' most important tools in keeping Negroes second-class citizens.

During Reconstruction, the South was forced to ratify Amendment XV to the United States Constitution, which declared, "The right of citizens of the United States to vote shall not be denied or abridged by the United States or by any state on account of race, color, or previous condition of servitude." Since the Amendment went into effect in 1870, Southern states have used various devices to defeat its purpose. These have included literacy tests, "grandfather" clauses, poll taxes, "white primaries," and difficult registration forms.

The grandfather clause was an attempt to keep illiterate Negroes disfranchised while enabling illiterate whites to vote. Such a clause stipulated that sons, grandsons, and all family descendants of persons eligible to vote before Reconstruction, need not pass a literacy test or meet property requirements before voting. Of course, few Negroes could vote before Reconstruction. Consequently, most Negroes were required to take difficult literacy tests. In addition to proving they could read and write, Negroes might be asked to interpret an obscure clause from a state constitution. Even the Negroes who had some educational opportunities could not pass these tests.

The white primary denied Negroes an opportunity to select a Democratic candidate. In a primary election, voters choose among nominees of a single party to select the one who will run in the general election. In the South, the winner of the Democratic primary was virtually assured victory in the general election, because the Republican vote was usually negligible. Thus, when Negroes were denied membership in the Democratic party or were prohibited by law from voting in the primary, they were in fact disfranchised.

However, most tactics of disfranchisement have been halted by court decisions and federal legislation. The grandfather clause was declared unconstitutional by the United States Supreme Court in 1915, and the white primary met the same fate in 1944. The federal Civil Rights Acts of 1957, 1960, and 1964 authorized the Department of Justice to assist Negroes in thwarting discrimination at the polls. The role of the Justice Department has been to institute lawsuits against state officials who impede the registration of Negro voters. Poll taxes were outlawed for federal elections in 1964 when Amendment XXIV to the Constitution was ratified. And in 1965, shortly after a protest march in Selma, Alabama, erupted in violence, the Voting Rights Act was passed. The law permitted federal officials to register Negroes who had been unfairly turned away by local officials. The act wiped out most of the tests used by Southern registrars to prevent blacks from voting.

Statistics reveal a great stride in the area of Negro suffrage. In 1932, out of an estimated 5,000,000 Negroes of voting age in twelve Southern states, only 100,000 could vote. By 1961, Southern Negro registration totaled 1,300,000. With the passage of the Voting Rights Act, accompanied by vigorous efforts by white and black organizations, more than 3,000,000 Southern Negroes registered to vote in 1969. Still, even that figure was less than 65 percent of all blacks eligible to vote. The figure for whites was over 80 percent. These statistics reflected a growing level of literacy in the South, but they also showed that much work remained to be done.

Why the interest in voting? Why have those seeking changes not concentrated solely on more pressing problems, such as the elimination of Jim Crow schools, segregated housing, or poverty? A Negro from Memphis, Tennessee, put it this way: "As I see it, Negro voting in the South will be the big cure to segregation. Freedom rides and lunch counter sit-ins may get more attention than knocking on doors and registering voters, but this [the right to vote] is basic to every other freedom."

In American society, political rights have often paved the way to other rights. Negro votes count. Once Negroes vote, the reasoning goes, white politicians will begin to care for the needs of black voters as eagerly as they do for others. And, more importantly, black voters will begin to elect black politicians to local, state, and national offices.

If there is widespread agreement—among friends as well as foes of Negroes—on the effectiveness of the right to vote as a force for the advancement of black people, what obstacles prevent Negroes from voting or using their votes effectively? How formidable are these obstacles? The two selections in this Problem explore these issues. In your reading, consider the following questions:

1 Will it be more advantageous to black voters in the South to ally themselves with white liberals or to work among themselves to elect black candidates? Use evidence from the readings to support your answer.

2 A Negro quoted in the introduction said, "Negro voting in the South will be the big cure to segregation." Do you agree? Explain your answer.

I

BLACK POLITICS IN ALABAMA

Because they met opposition from local white politicians in the Democratic party, Negroes in Lowndes County, Alabama, decided to form their own party and use a black panther as their symbol. Why they did so was explained by the party's chairman, John Hulett, in a speech in Los Angeles in 1966.   ☐ Abridgement of "How the Black Panther Party was Organized" by John Hulett from *The Black Panther Party*. Reprinted by permission of Merit Publishers, 1966. Pp. 7-15.

. . . Some time ago, we organized a political group of our own known as the Lowndes County Freedom Organization, whose emblem is the Black Panther.

We were criticized, we were called communists, we were called everything else, black nationalists and what not, because we did this. Any group which starts at a time like this to speak out for what is right—they are going to be ridiculed. The people of Lowndes County realized this. Today we are moving further.

Too long Negroes have been begging, especially in the South, for things they should be working for. So the people in Lowndes County decided to organize themselves—to go out and work for the things we wanted in life—not only for the people in Lowndes County, but for every county in the state of Alabama, in the Southern states . . . .

In Lowndes County, there is a committee in the Democratic Party. This committee not only controls the courthouse, it controls the entire county. When they found out that the Negroes were going to run candidates in the primary of the Democratic Party on May 3, they assembled themselves together and began to talk about what they were going to do. Knowing this is one of the poorest counties in the nation, what they decided to do was change the registration fees in the county.

Two years ago, if a person wanted to run for sheriff, tax collector or tax assessor, all he had to do was pay $50 and then he qualified to be the candidate. This year, the entrance fee is about $900. If a person wants to run, he has to pay $500 to run for office. In the primary, when they get through cheating and stealing, then the candidate is eliminated. So we decided that we wouldn't get into such a primary because we were tired of being tricked by the Southern whites. After forming our own political group today, we feel real strong. We feel that we are doing the right thing in Lowndes County.

We have listened to everybody who wanted to talk, we listened to them speak, but one thing we had to learn for ourselves. As a group of people, we must think for ourselves and act on our own accord. And this we have done.

Through the years, Negroes in the South have been going for the bones while whites have been going for the meat. The Negroes of Lowndes County today are tired of the bones—we are going to have some of the meat too.

At the present time, we have our own candidates who have been nominated by the Lowndes County Freedom Organization. And we fear that this might not be enough to avoid the tricks that are going to be used in Lowndes County against us.

In Lowndes County, the sheriff is the custodian of the court-house. . . .

After talking to the sheriff about having the use of the courthouse lawn for our mass nominating meeting, not the courthouse but just the lawn, he refused to give the Negroes permission. We reminded him that last year in August, that one of the biggest Klan rallies that has ever been held in the state of Alabama was held on this lawn of this courthouse. And he gave them permission. . . .

But he would not permit Negroes to have the use of the court-house. For one thing he realized that we would build a party—and if he could keep us from forming our own political group then we would always stand at the feet of the Southern whites and of the Democratic Party. So we told him that we were going to have this meeting, we were going to have it here, on the courthouse lawn. And we wouldn't let anybody scare us off. We told him, we won't expect you to protect us, and if you don't, Negroes will protect themselves.

Then we asked him a second time to be sure he understood what we were saying. We repeated it to him the second time. And then we said to him, Sheriff, if you come out against the people, then we are going to arrest you.

And he said, I will not give you permission to have this meeting here. I can't protect you from the community.

Then we reminded him that according to the law of the state of Alabama, that this mass meeting which was set up to nominate our candidates must be held in or around a voters' polling place. And if we decide to hold it a half a mile away from the courthouse, some in-dividual would come up and protest our mass meeting. And our elec-tion would be thrown out.

So we wrote the Justice Department and told them what was going to happen in Lowndes County.

All of a sudden the Justice Department started coming in fast into the county. They said to me, John, what is going to happen next Tuesday at the courthouse?

I said, We are going to have our mass meeting. And he wanted to know where. And I said on the lawn of the courthouse.

He said, I thought the sheriff had told you you couldn't come there. And I said, Yes, but we are going to be there.

Then he wanted to know, if shooting takes place, what are we going to do. And I said, that we are going to stay out here and everybody die together.

And then he began to get worried, and I said, Don't worry. You're going to have to be here to see it out and there's no place to hide, so whatever happens, you can be a part of it.

And then he began to really panic. And he said, There's nothing I can do.

And I said, I'm not asking you to do anything. All I want you to know is we are going to have a mass meeting. If the sheriff cannot protect us, then we are going to protect ourselves. And I said to him, through the years in the South, Negroes have never had any protection, and today we aren't looking to anybody to protect us. We are going to protect ourselves.

That was on Saturday. On Sunday, at about 2 o'clock, we were having a meeting, and we decided among ourselves that we were going to start collecting petitions for our candidates to be sure that they got on the ballot. The state laws require at least 25 signatures of qualified electors and so we decided to get at least 100 for fear somebody might come up and find fault. And we decided to still have our mass meeting and nominate our candidates.

About 2:30, here comes the Justice Department again, and he was really worried. And he said he wasn't satisfied. He said to me, John, I've done all I can do, and I don't know what else I can do, and now it looks like you'll have to call this meeting off at the courthouse.

And I said, We're going to have it.

He stayed around for awhile and then got in his car and drove off, saying, I'll see you tomorrow, maybe. And we stayed at this meeting from 2:30 until about 11:30 that night. About 11:15, the Justice Department came walking up the aisle of the church and said to me, Listen. I've talked to the Attorney General of the state of Alabama, and he said that you can go ahead and have a mass meeting at the church and it will be legal.

Then we asked him, Do you have any papers that say that's true, that are signed by the Governor or the Attorney General? And he said no. And we said to him, Go back and get it legalized, and bring it back here to us and we will accept it.

. . . [On] Monday at 3 o'clock, I went to the courthouse and there in the sheriff's office were the papers all legalized and fixed up, saying that we could go to the church to have our mass meeting.

To me, this showed strength. When people are together, they can do a lot of things, but when you are alone you cannot do anything.

There are 600 Negroes in the county who did not trust in themselves and who joined the Democratic Party. We warned the entire state of Alabama that running on the Democratic ticket could not do them any good, because this party is controlled by people like [George] Wallace; and whoever won would have to do what these people said to do.

Now, to me, the Democratic Party primaries and the Democratic Party is something like an integrated gambler who carries a card around in his pocket and every now and then he has to let somebody win to keep the game going. To me, this is what the Democratic Party means to the people in Alabama. It's a gambling game. And somebody's got to win to keep the game going every now and then. . . .

I would like to say here, and this is one thing I am proud of, the people in Lowndes County stood together, and the 600 people who voted in the Democratic primary have realized one thing, that they were tricked by the Democratic Party. And now they too are ready to join us with the Lowndes County Freedom Organization whose emblem is the black panther.

We have seven people who are running for office this year in our county; namely, the coroner, three members of the board of education —and if we win those three, we will control the board of education —tax collector, tax assessor, and the individual who carries a gun at his side, the sheriff. . . .

I would like to let the people here tonight know why we chose this black panther as our emblem. Many people have been asking this question for a long time. Our political group is open to whoever wants to come in, who would like to work with us. But we aren't begging anyone to come in. It's open, you come, at your own free will and accord.

But this black panther is a vicious animal, as you know. He never bothers anything, but when you start pushing him he moves backwards, backwards, and backwards into his corner, and then he comes out to destroy everything that's before him.

Negroes in Lowndes County have been pushed back through the years. We have been deprived of our rights to speak, to move, and to do whatever we want to do at all times. And now we are going to start moving. On November 8 of this year, we plan to take over the courthouse in Hayneville. And whatever it takes to do it, we're going to do it.

We've decided to stop begging. We've decided to stop asking for integration. Once we control the courthouse, once we control the board of education, we can build our school system where our boys and girls can get an education in Lowndes County. There are 89 prominent families in this county who own 90 percent of the land. These people will be taxed. And we will collect these taxes. And if they don't pay them, we'll take their property and sell it to whoever wants to buy it. And we know there will be people who will buy land where at the present time they cannot buy it. This is what it's going to take.

We aren't asking any longer for protection — we won't need it — or for anyone to come from the outside to speak for us, because we're going to speak for ourselves now and from now on. And I think not only in Lowndes County, not only in the state of Alabama, not only in the South, but in the North — I hope they too will start thinking for themselves. And that they will move and join us in this fight for freedom.

II

"WE'VE GOT A LOT TO LEARN"

Although there was an all-out effort in 1968 to register South Carolina Negroes, the results were less than satisfying, especially in the fall elections. ☐ "South Carolina" by Pat Watters from *The Atlantic Monthly* (September 1968). Copyright © 1968, by The Atlantic Monthly Company, Boston, Mass. Reprinted by permission. Pp. 20-28.

In September, 1967, names of every registered voter in the state were wiped off the books, and the electorate was required to reregister; this occurs every 10 years by state law. Whites, accustomed to the nuisance, took it in stride. But for Negroes, it was the occasion for renewal of a crusade: the old, anguished struggle to register voters. Now it is near success in much of the South, but only a few years ago registration was one of the most difficult and dangerous activities of the Southern civil rights movement. Negroes went to work across the state with registration meetings (often in churches), with canvassing, with registration booths at shópping centers, pool halls, dances, churches, wherever people gathered; in Columbia at a large car wash. . . .

Most of the registration effort was coordinated by the South Carolina Voter Education Project, a confederation of registration organizations formed in 1962–1963, the first such in the South. James L. Felder, twenty-seven, a graduate of Howard University Law School and a native of Sumter, directs the organization, and financial help comes from the Voter Education Project of the Southern Regional Council. . . .

. . . Instructions were sent out, workshops were held on procedure, and Negroes by the hundreds turned out for precinct meetings, often outnumbering the more or less professional whites who bother with such things, and capturing many of the organizations. More than 5000 Negroes participated in precinct organization meetings in 28 counties and elected 182 Negro officers. Twelve hundred were named delegates to county conventions where they elected 78 Negro officers, and 175 were delegates to the state convention. There they elected no Negro officers but did get 5 Negroes named as delegates and 4 as alternate delegates to the Democratic National Convention.

One of the delegates was George Holman, a fifty-nine-year-old undertaker in Moncks Corner. A short, modest man, he continued to canvass daily for registration as chairman of the local voter organization. He drove deep into surrounding rural areas to call on farms and cabins miles apart from each other. . . . He said the success with party organizations had encouraged many Negroes in his area to register for the first time. "People are beginning to see it will work. Our people have been so far from politics. They were never told about it. It is like Greek to them. But if you get them person to person and begin to explain it, you'll see them light up, and they'll say, 'Oh, I get it.'"

There were sad stories of how, more than once, Negroes with a majority at a precinct meeting would be talked into a compromise on offices by the whites, a Negro getting a ceremonial one like chairman, and whites holding on to the powerful one of committeeman. "These damn white boys have been playing this game of politics for three hundred years," said a Charleston leader. "We've just been in it since 1948. We've been learning. But we've got a lot to learn."

Heartened by the success in party organization affairs, and perhaps as part of the enthusiasm of the reregistration drive, more Negro candidates qualified for the June 11 Democratic primary than at any other time in recent history. . . .

The maxim [saying] that Negro candidates spur Negro registration was reinforced by the efforts of candidates themselves to register people. . . .

Little attention was paid to the Negro reregistration effort until the South Carolina Secretary of State's office, responding to requests, reported results through February 24. Negroes had, it was announced, outregistered whites in seven counties. . . . In those counties particularly, and in the state generally, the news stirred white registration efforts. Booths began to appear in shopping center parking lots in white sections. Deputy registrars showed up with forms at civic clubs (the Southern affiliates are still generally all white), and at factories. Radio, television, and newspaper advertising urging reregistration increased. . . .

Final results announced after the May 11 cutoff indicated, however, that white registration had declined from 730,000 in 1967 to 566,271. Negro registration, 24.4 percent of the total, stood at 182,514 — still less than 50 percent of the potential, and lowest on this score in 1968 in all of the South. Moreover, in no county did Negroes emerge with a voting majority, not even in . . . [those] with majority Negro voting-age populations.

The ensuing primary was more disappointing to Negro hopes than the registration figures would have augured. Of 31 Negro candidates for local offices (county council, board of education, superintendent of education, magistrate, coroner), only 10 survived runoffs. Ten of the 12 legislative candidates were defeated. The other 2 lost in runoffs. George A. Payton, Negro attorney of Charleston, who challenged ultra-hawk Mendel Rivers, campaigned against him on a platform including the peace issue. Payton, with about one third of his district Negro, had hoped to see the white vote split between Republicans and Democrats. . . . But perhaps even more bitter were returns showing considerable Negro support going to supersegregationist Rivers. One explanation was that they feared losing Charleston's outsized version of the military-industrial complex, for which Rivers has claimed credit.

Part of Payton's problem was less than enthusiastic support (if not covert opposition) from some Negro leaders. Division of Negro leaders' support helped account for defeats of at least two other congressional candidates and one senatorial challenger who had notions of welding Negro and working-class white votes. . . .

The other Southern states have had the same experience of finding it more difficult to elect Negro or Negro-favored candidates than to register formidable Negro voting strength. The common causes are honest choice of whites by Negro voters, fraud or intimidation at the polls, and the casting of imperfect ballots by people not yet accustomed to the process.

There is obvious danger if Southern Negroes continue to see all the hope they have built up in the ballot disappointed. One statistic in South Carolina seems ominous. Despite all the political activity and the reregistration campaign, only 55 percent of all those Negroes who were reached by the campaign turned out to vote in the primary. . . . And there must be taken into account the dispiriting effect of the assassinations of Dr. Martin Luther King, Jr., and Senator Robert Kennedy, as well as the national drift toward riot and repression.

PROBLEM 13

Northern Politics and the Black

Black mayors of large cities in 1970? Anyone making that prediction twenty years before would have been laughed at. But by mid-1970, three cities—Cleveland, Ohio; Gary, Indiana; and Newark, New Jersey—had elected black mayors to cope with the problems of urban living. There also were increasing numbers of black legislators, both at the state and national levels, making laws for millions of citizens, white and black.

The previous Problem described the struggle to win the right to vote for black citizens in the South. This Problem deals with questions of black political power in Northern states, where Negroes generally have been able to vote, but where black votes have been manipulated by white politicians.

During the 1960's, black politicians began to use their power in a more direct way. Two developments were influential in creating a new political atmosphere. First, continuing migration of whites from cities to suburbs increased the percentage of black voters from urban areas. This increase has been enough to control the outcomes of elections in some cities, and statistics indicate that the trend will continue. Among the cities predicted to gain Negro population majorities by the 1980's are New Orleans, Baltimore, Jacksonville (Fla.), St. Louis, Philadelphia, Oakland (Calif.), Atlanta, and Chicago.

The second development concerns the political implications of the slogan *black power*. Black politicians know they must answer the demands of the militants for faster relief of many social and economic problems, including the demand for greater Negro control of programs designed to help the ghetto.

Of course, the first challenge a black politician must meet is getting himself elected. This involves a serious choice of strategies: Should a black politician organize a separate political party to challenge the white "establishment," or should he or she seek white allies and build political coalitions? After a successful election, this choice of strategies remains, as a mayor (or other elected official) builds a staff in hopes of fulfilling campaign promises.

This Problem focuses on two aspects of Negro politics: the election and the performance in office. The first reading describes how Carl Stokes won a primary battle and his election as the first black mayor of Cleveland, Ohio. The second reading outlines the problems and performances of black mayors in four cities. Think about these questions as you read:

1 From what segments of the population did Carl Stokes get support?

2 What problems do the mayors discussed in Reading II have in common?

3 What is meant by the statement in Reading II, "America will still be electing black mayors before it elects mayors who happen to be black"?

4 On the basis of what you have read, how is a black mayor a man caught in the middle? What groups regularly criticize him?

I

BLACK POLITICS IN CLEVELAND

In 1967, Carl Stokes became the first black man to win the office of mayor in Cleveland, Ohio. In 1965, he had run as an independent, but lost to Ralph Locher, the Democratic candidate. When he ran again in 1967, this time as a Democrat, Stokes first had to defeat the incumbent Mayor Locher in a primary race. This article, by three professors at Case Western Reserve University in Cleveland, describes the primary battle. ☐ Jeffrey K. Hadden, Louis H. Masotti, and Victor Thiessen. "The Making of the Negro Mayors 1967," Transaction, January-February 1968, Pp. 22-24.

It was in the 1965 Democratic primary that the first signs of a "black bloc" vote emerged. The Negroes, who had previously supported incumbent Democratic mayoral candidates, if not enthusiastically at least consistently, made a concerted effort to dump Locher. . . . There were two reasons.

Locher had supported his police chief after the latter had made some tactless remarks about Negroes. Incensed Negro leaders demanded an audience with the mayor, and when he refused, his office was the scene of demonstrations, sit-ins, and arrests. At that point, as one of the local reporters put it, "Ralph Locher became a dirty name in the ghetto."

Stokes, as an independent, and his supporters hoped that the Democratic primary would eliminate the *stronger* candidate, Locher. For then a black bloc would have a good chance of deciding the general election because of an even split in the white vote.

Despite the Negro community's efforts, Locher won the primary and went on to narrowly defeat Stokes. . . .

Although he made a strong showing in defeat, Carl Stokes's political future looked bleak. No one expected the Democratic leaders to give Stokes another opportunity to win by means of a split vote. Nor were there other desirable elected offices Stokes could seek. . . . So, in 1966, Stokes sought re-election to the state House unopposed.

Between 1965 and 1967, Cleveland went from bad to worse, physically, socially, and financially. With no other immediate possibilities, Stokes began to think about running for mayor again. The big question was whether to risk taking on Locher in the primary — or to file as an independent again.

In effect, Stokes's decision was made for him. Seth Taft, slated to be the Republican candidate, told Stokes he would withdraw from the election entirely if Stokes filed as an independent in order to gain the advantage of a three-man general election. Taft had concluded that his best strategy was to face a Negro, *alone*, or a faltering incumbent, *alone*, in the general election. But not both. In a three-man race with Locher and Stokes, Taft correctly assumed that he would be the man in the middle with no chance for victory. . . .

Meanwhile, Locher committed blunder after blunder—and Democratic party leaders began to question whether he could actually win another election. In the weeks before filing for the primary, Democratic leaders even pressured Locher to accept a Federal judgeship and clear the way for the president of the city council to run. . . . When Locher refused to withdraw, the party reluctantly rallied behind him. . . .

Now, in 1965 Stokes had received only about 6000 white votes in the city in a 239,000 voter turnout. To win in the primary, he had to enlarge and consolidate the Negro vote—and increase his white support on the westside and in the eastside ethnic wards.

The first part of his strategy was a massive voter-registration drive in the Negro wards—to reinstate the potential Stokes voters dropped from the rolls for failing to vote since the 1964 Presidential election. The Stokes organization—aided by Martin Luther King Jr. and the Southern Christian Leadership Conference, as well as by a grant (in part earmarked for voter registration) from the Ford Foundation to the Cleveland chapter of CORE—did succeed in registering many Negroes. But there was a similar drive mounted by the Democratic Party on behalf of Locher. . . .

The second part of the Stokes strategy took him across the polluted Cuyahoga River into the white wards that had given him a mere 3 per cent of the vote in 1965. He spoke wherever he would be received—to small groups in private homes, in churches, and in public and private halls. While he was not always received enthusiastically, he did not confront many hostile crowds. He faced the race issue squarely and encouraged his audience to judge him on his ability.

Stokes's campaign received a big boost when the *Plain Dealer*, the largest daily in Ohio, endorsed him. Next, the *Cleveland Press* called for a change in City Hall, but declined to endorse . . . Stokes. . . .

More people voted in this primary than in any other in Cleveland's history. When the ballots were counted, Stokes had 52.5 per cent of the votes—he had defeated Locher by a plurality of 18,000 votes. . . .

What produced Stokes's clear victory? . . . The decisive factor was the size of the Negro turnout. While Negroes constituted only about 40 per cent of the voters, 73.4 per cent of them turned out, compared with only 58.4 per cent of the whites. Predominantly Negro wards cast 96.2 per cent of their votes for Stokes. . . .

Newspaper and magazine reports of the primary election proclaimed that Stokes could not have won without the white vote. Our own estimate—based on matching wards with census tracts, and allowing for only slight shifts in racial composition in some wards since the 1965 special census—is that Stokes received 16,000 white votes. His margin of victory was 18,000. . . . Thus Stokes's inroad into the white vote was not the decisive factor in his primary victory, although it was important.

II

HOW TO RUN A CITY

This article describes how four black mayors organized their governments and tried to bring much-needed help to their cities. ☐ Abridgement of "The Black Mayors" from *Newsweek* (August 3, 1970). Copyright Newsweek, Inc., 1970, and used by permission. Pp. 16-17, 18, 21-22.

Kenneth Allen Gibson is a pleasantly plump civil engineer with a calm, careful approach to life that he cultivated as a child in the city's Central Ward ghetto. Gibson is also Newark's new mayor and the latest initiate in a small but steadily growing fraternity of black mayors in big Northern cities. The list now includes Carl Stokes in Cleveland, Richard Hatcher in Gary, Indiana, and Walter E. Washington in Washington, D.C. And it is growing. By the mid-1980s, according to current population estimates, the number of sizable U.S. cities with black majorities will have grown from three to thirteen—and at least as many more will have black votes enough, in coalition with liberal whites, to elect Negro mayors. "The cities really represent the beachhead for black political power," says Gary's Mayor Hatcher —and, like other American minorities before them, the blacks have begun to claim the cities as their own.

The stakes are far more than skin-deep; the cities, even as the emerging Negro majorities inherit them, are struggling for their very survival, and the current crop of black mayors has accepted this as the main challenge. So far they have grappled manfully and sometimes imaginatively with the problems of urban blight, social tension and psychic despond. But, like their white colleagues, they have learned that their grandest dreams must often be deferred while they settle for whatever diminished projects and programs they can get in a time of tight money and tenuous hope on the urban frontier. . . .

The parade of ethnic groups into city halls across the country has usually been a rousing urban success story, with fat contracts, patronage jobs and blossoming public-works projects in the old neighborhood as the bounty. When the Irish or the Italians took hold of a city, it seemed somehow irrefutably theirs. But history has played another of its cruel jokes on the Negroes: the mantle of power, now finally within their reach, may no longer be adequate to the problems that come with it. Running any big city today is a man-killing labor; by the time a city has come to the point of electing a black mayor, the task may in fact be nearly impossible. A black majority, or something close to it, means that successful whites have fled, taking with them much of the solid, middle-class economic base upon which all cities depend—and leaving behind white, working-class families who can neither flee nor easily adjust to social change. Depleted municipal revenues are quickly overrun by increased demands for services from the groups that remain; the bills for health, welfare, transit and police protection spiral. Everything conspires to limit what the new black mayor can do. But no similar limits have been imposed on what people—especially black people—expect from him. . . .

Gibson, like his confreres in Cleveland, Gary and Washington, has tried in his own way to cope; each of the mayors stays in touch with the others by periodic phone calls and meetings. Sometimes they exchange tips; Hatcher, for example, suggested that Gibson get started immediately trying to make friends on his white-dominated city council. (Gibson did, inviting the councilmen one by one to his house; some of them had never set foot in a mayor's home before.) And sometimes the black mayors commiserate. Their record thus far is mixed—victories tend to run small; defeats are frequent and frustrating. The record to date:

When he first strode into Cleveland's City Hall three years ago, Carl Burton Stokes was all wide smiles and self-assurance. Now he tends, to slump behind his desk. Gone is the "up feeling" that followed Stokes's election and helped attract $5.6 million in private contributions to his "Cleveland: Now!" civic reconstruction program. Around town now, there is a feeling of frustration and even bitterness. "I never dreamed—I just never dreamed of the day-to-day crisis environment in which a mayor lives," says Stokes. "There aren't any textbooks."

On the surface, the handsome, 43-year-old mayor still seems to be Cleveland's coolest cat. "I don't think anyone on our staff has seen him in the same suit twice," chuckles a local newspaper editor. And he has had his share of major achievements: early on he snared a hefty bundle of Federal urban renewal funds (with some help from President Lyndon Johnson), and today he claims credit for 5,000 new units of public housing—60 per cent more than the city had put up in the 30 years before his arrival in City Hall. But the demand for public money today vastly exceeds the supply, and Stokes is hurting. Only last week he had to propose doubling the city's payroll tax just to cover municipal pay raises and abort a series of near-paralyzing public-employee strikes.

In the absence of a healthy bankroll, Stokes has had to settle for smaller gestures of concern. He has taken to personal strolls through Cleveland's strictly divided ethnic communities where he occasionally dazzles neighborhood pool sharks with his own cue-stick virtuosity. He turned a downtown square into a popular outdoor restaurant and cleaned up small areas of polluted Lake Erie to serve as makeshift swimming pools for children. "Little things can be done to make city life more bearable," he says.

Flak: Some critics complain that Stokes has been overly intimate with Cleveland's militants; they have never forgiven him for pulling white policemen out of the Glenville ghetto in the tindery wake of a shoot-out between the cops and a band of black nationalists two years ago. Stokes does keep lines open to the militants, but the relationship is considerably less ardent than some whites imagine. "I don't think Stokes has much interest in black revolution," says one of its practitioners. "He just gets along with everybody. What's wrong with that?" . . .

Richard Hatcher is the prototypical straight arrow—a church-going, 37-year-old bachelor who neither drinks nor smokes and whose only identifiable vice is an occasional game of Ping Pong. When he became mayor of Gary three years ago—despite a blatantly racist opposition campaign—Hatcher immediately mounted a puritanical clean-up crusade that transformed Indiana's notoriously corrupt "Sin City" into a comparatively antiseptic urban laboratory.

The change of image—along with the publicity attending Hatcher's election as the first black mayor of a predominantly black Northern city—opened doors to a wide range of executive suites, foundation vaults and Federal funding agencies. More than $86 million in public and private funds flowed in to assist Hatcher's scandal-free administration, and the results include 3,000 units of low- and middle-income housing (Gary's first in a decade), massive job-training and placement programs and several imaginative educational experiments. Moreover, in an era of corporate flight from the cities, U.S. Steel, the mainstay of Gary's economy, and other local firms have decided to stay and help pay the price of progress. And within the administration, urban specialists, some of them subsidized by private funds, have instituted money-saving efficiencies (including the previously unheard-of practice of competitive bidding) and developed a genius for mining the available sources of cash. "If it had been simply a matter of my blackness," says Hatcher, "we wouldn't still be getting these funds after two years."

But Gary's sorest problems — the billowing smog from its factories and the continuing crime on its streets — have defied solution despite the application of cash. And the money itself has brought Hatcher new political problems: most of it comes earmarked for the city's poor — and that generally means the blacks. "Working-class whites are getting angry because they need services, too," admits a City Hall aide. Hatcher has made a concentrated effort to maintain good relations with Gary's polyglot white community, attending weddings, socials and Sunday morning services there as well as in black neighborhoods. . . .

The basic problem in political science troubling Washington, D.C., is almost as old as the Republic itself. From the first, the city was organized as a special, stateless District of Columbia, almost totally dependent upon the U.S. Congress for everything from its annual budget to criminal ordinances. The intent was to save the nation's capital from falling prey to any narrow sectional interest; the result was that a busy city of 827,600 inhabitants — 70 per cent of them blacks — now finds itself at the mercy of a score or more legislators whose various interests (a segregationist constituency back home, for example) have little to do with the district's pressing needs.

As Washington's Presidentially appointed chief executive, Walter E. Washington is, consequently, cast in the unique role of mayor as middleman, lobbyist and diplomat. "To be mayor of Washington," concedes a key aide on the Senate's District committee, "you have to achieve your goals by guile, wile and good offices."

Fortunately for him, Washington started learning the ropes early in Washington's labyrinthine bureaucracy. While still a student at Howard University, not far from the White House, he caught on as an intern with the National Capital Housing Authority and labored there with quiet competence for twenty years. His low-profiled virtues finally boosted him to prominence as executive director there and later as chairman of New York City's giant Housing Authority. In 1967, he was summoned by President Lyndon Johnson to serve as mayor-commissioner of a newly reorganized and slightly more emancipated district government. In the riots that followed the assassination of Martin Luther King Jr., and through a subsequent succession of minor crises and confrontations, Washington demonstrated a stolid un-flappability and an engaging talent for dealing with local business-men, moderates and militants as well as visiting demonstrators.

Plague: Mayor Washington and his highly regarded police chief, Jerry Wilson, have helped soothe the city's riot jitters by cutting down the number of police incidents that classically cause riots. But crime in the streets plagues the mayor nonetheless. . . .

And there are other grumbles: some critics fault the mayor for administrative bungling (in housing starts, slumlord prosecutions, preparation of reports) and a lack of passion in lobbying on Capitol Hill (where his budget request was cut by one-quarter). "I'm not a table pounder," replies Washington, who is burly but still somehow rather boyish at 55. "You can big-mouth the situation and lose the whole ball game." In a way, of course, all the carping is something of a compliment, for it indicates that he has transformed what might well have been a figurehead office into one from which people actually ex-pect results. Even a Southern congressman who used to make a point of addressing him, correctly but demeaningly, as "mayor-commis-sioner" has lately taken to calling Walter Washington "Mr. Mayor."

Kenneth Gibson has learned from all of them. He has spent his first weeks trying to show an even-handed concern for expectant blacks and suspicious whites. He asked Newark's ex-fire director John Pershing Caufield, 51, a white leader who supported him during a bitter run-off campaign, to resume his old post. He named a veteran white cop, John Redden, to head the police department and he in-vited old City Hall politico Donald Malafronte to stay on as an urban affairs specialist. The choices irritated some of Gibson's color-conscious black supporters, but he softened the pain by naming blacks and Puerto Ricans to other key City Hall and school-board vacancies.

The balancing act seemed to work: the mayor was greeted with nearly equal warmth in the city's white and black neighborhoods last week in a tour promoting cooperation with the 1970 census. He is trying, moreover, to program some modest projects that can be carried out at once with maximum show at minimum cost: a city-wide clean-up campaign and new street lights. "It is important that the people see some changes—not just a new mayor," says Gibson.

The change of faces alone does hold out some hope for Newark. Gibson, merely by turning out ex-Mayor Hugh Addonizio's scandal-streaked administration, won entrée with businessmen, foundation executives and state officials who had hung back while the old crowd controlled the till. There have been other tokens as well; four local corporation executives, on leave from their own jobs, are working gratis for Gibson, and they are the backbone of his fledgling administration.

Leverage: But Newark is desperate for cash, and business is considerably less keen on the remedy Gibson favors: a payroll tax on the 300,000 suburban commuters who flood into town daily. When businessmen object, Gibson invites them to come up with an alternative tax package; he suspects that none exists. And he is not at all above horse trading—or arm twisting—to get just what he wants. Newark, notes one aide slyly, is a main supplier of water to several surrounding suburbs—a fact of life that may make them, and their legislators, more attentive to what the city needs. And Gibson himself is counting on his own leverage as the mayor of the biggest city in an Eastern swing state. The office in Newark is nonpartisan, and Gibson, to maximize his maneuverability, resists taking a party label. "In 1972, there will be a Presidential election," he grins, "and I'll still be in office."

Gibson will need all the leverage—and all the help—he can get. Addonizio didn't want to raise taxes before the election and so stuck Gibson with a $21 million gap in the city's education budget; Gibson will have to raise it quickly, or the schools won't open in September [they did open September 9, 1970]. And beyond the school crisis he must find ways to cope with a staggering array of problems that make Newark a classic example of urban disaster. A third of the city's housing is substandard, the crime rate is one of the highest in the nation and black unemployment stands at a recession-level 11 per cent. City Hall salaries are so low ($20,000 is top dollar for most departmental portfolios) that executive-grade talent is nearly impossible to hire.

Gibson even travels in a run-down, city-owned Cadillac because trading it in for a new Caddy would be an extravagance ("Imagine what the papers would say") and his own economy alternative—a Checker —was hooted down by aides as too plain for his high station.

"Mr. Mayor" is no longer an uncommon title for black men: there are more than 50 Negro mayors in the U.S., though most reign in all-black or mostly black small towns far from the cities people mean when they talk about the "urban crisis." . . .

. . . The politics of change thus far has been a politics of color, pitting working-class whites against the blacks and their middle-class, white-liberal allies along lines as sharp as the old politics of party has always been in the cities. The cities seem to survive the transition, but the pain reproduces itself; urban America will still be electing black mayors before it elects mayors who happen to be black.

Sensitivity: And for a mayor, there is little redeeming magic in blackness. Most of the Negroes currently in office tend to downplay its importance. They do contend that color gives them a special sensitivity to the problems of black constituencies. "I'm really very reluctant to even say this out loud," Gary's Hatcher told an interviewer, "but we haven't had a serious or a major disorder in the last two years." No black mayor, however, would be so bold as to offer himself as a guarantee against rioting; none of them yet knows how deep the euphoria of the blacks' accession to power runs, or how long it will last.

Like the others, Ken Gibson denies any magic touch with the militants. But already he had delicately defused his first potential riot. . . . [The] experience of Stokes in Cleveland and Hatcher in Gary is that a black mayor who is competent and diligent enough can gradually erode white resistance and even win white support. Accessibility is important; it remains a sad truth that a black mayor must constantly put himself on display to demonstrate that he does not carry a spear in one hand and a Molotov cocktail in the other. "The job of mayor has become highly personal in nature," says Carl Stokes, and he has developed a gift for the personal touch. Once he materialized a playground for a white neighborhood that had needed one for years. Getting it counted; opening it in person seemed to count for even more. "The mayor himself came down here," said one awed white woman. "And you know—he shook my hand. That's the first time I've ever shaked a mayor's hand."

Gibson, too, values the direct approach; he will see practically anyone who asks for an audience, the most arrant pests included, for at least ten minutes, and he is negotiating TV and radio talk shows to get his message across. And the message, like Gibson himself, will be simple and straightforward. He will promise little, because he understands that — barring some dazzling reordering of the nation's priorities — no big-city mayor, black or white, is likely to be able to do very much. And yet, like his brother black mayors, he seems invincibly determined to keep the faith. "I have," he says, "a great deal of faith in my own ability to perform. And I also have a great deal of faith in our system to respond. The system can stand a great deal of improvement. But nobody has shown me a better one."

PROBLEM 14

New Patterns of Negro Leadership

American Negroes experienced a revolution after 1945, a revolution in expectations. Following World War II, the steady movement toward first-class citizenship for black people quickened, with significant actions taking place in courts of law, in voting booths, in restaurants, and in the streets of the nation.

A decade of intense civil rights activity was launched in 1954 when the United States Supreme Court declared segregated schools to be unconstitutional. In 1955, Dr. Martin Luther King, Jr. effectively organized the Negroes of Atlanta, Georgia, in a bus boycott. The boycott lasted two years, and when it was over, Negroes no longer were degraded by being forced to sit or stand in the rear of buses.

In 1960, a group of black college students decided that they, as well as white persons, had the right to eat at a lunch counter in Greensboro, North Carolina. This sit-in sparked an aggressive national movement and, in the next few years, thousands of young men and women—black and white, North and South—overturned local laws and customs that had maintained the institution of Jim Crow. Sit-ins, pray-ins, wade-ins, freedom rides, freedom marches, and demonstrations to open all schools to black children took place across the nation.

Perhaps the most inspiring demonstration took place in August 1963, when 200,000 black and white persons participated in the March on Washington. It was here that Dr. King eloquently expressed the prevailing goal of the movement: "I have a dream that my four little children will one day live in a nation where they will not be judged by the color of their skin but by the content of their character." The goals of the demonstrators were integration, equal rights, dignity, and respect; their methods, heavily influenced by Dr. King, were non-violent.

But discrimination against blacks and the persecution of black and white civil rights workers continued. The pages of history show snarling dogs, bombed out churches, the ghastly facts of the murders of three civil rights workers in Mississippi, the rage of white mothers outside schools being integrated, and howling white university students angry at the admission of but one Negro to "their" school.

The historical record also shows that Congress passed civil rights acts in 1957, 1960, 1964, and 1966, the Voting Rights Act of 1965, and the Fair Housing Act of 1968. These came in rapid succession, but not without struggle and sacrifice. However, the masses of black poor people were untouched by civil rights legislation, judicial decisions, and demonstrations. Passing laws, while providing protection and opening closed doors, did not put food in the mouths of black children.

The civil rights movement of the late 1950's and early 1960's revealed Southern injustice and violence, but did little to attack Northern injustice in dozens of black ghettos. It took riots, such as those in Watts, Chicago, Detroit, and Washington, D.C., to reveal the complex and deep-seated problems found in urban areas, problems that civil rights acts or sit-ins or marches could not solve.

The anger of black Americans was further inflamed when, in 1968, Dr. King was assassinated. Even before this tragic event, the mood of many Negro Americans had shifted from militant support of integration to militant pride in their race, pride in being black. The term "black power" seemed to shout that the right to eat a hamburger with a white man was no longer enough. The phrase "We shall overcome" was replaced by "Black is beautiful."

New groups did not always care to use the courts or Congress or nonviolent demonstrations. Violent words crept into the speeches of young black leaders and, in some cases, words turned into deeds.

How did Negro leaders react to this vigorous challenge by the young and the poor? Old-line organizations, such as the National Association for the Advancement of Colored People and the Urban League, came under heavy criticism because their tactics seemed so slow and outdated to the young militants, such as members of the Black Panther Party.

The old arguments of integration or separation, violence or non-violence—arguments that Negro leaders such as Douglass, Du Bois, Washington, and others had struggled with earlier—were again being debated. The selections that follow deal with the response of black leadership and the development of new leaders. As you read, consider these questions.

1　Why might young black militants consider Wilkins' speech (Reading I) outdated?

2　What did Malcolm X (Reading II) mean by the term "black nationalism"? Where might Malcolm X stand on black politics (Problem 13)?

3　Which parts of the Black Panther program, if any, seem unrealistic? Which ones could lead to violence? Which parts of the program do you agree with? Explain your answers.

4　What differences do you see among the goals and methods of Roy Wilkins, Malcolm X, and the Black Panther Party?

5　What is the future of black leadership, according to Reading IV? *Can* or *should* there be one leader of all Negroes in the United States? Why or why not?

I

A FLEXIBLE APPROACH

In 1964, Roy Wilkins, who was Executive Secretary of the National Association for the Advancement of Colored People, saw the civil rights movement in broad perspective. He said that tactics must be varied and flexible to serve the different types of Negro communities in the nation.　☐ Abridged from "We Must Use Every Tool," by Roy Wilkins. New South, XVIII, 2 (February 1964). Reprinted by permission of Roy Wilkins.

It may be that the time has now arrived when the civil rights forces need to go to a quarterback clinic. The goal of a football team is to make points enough to win the game. If points cannot be made with touchdowns, field goals can be called upon. If the line of opposition is unyielding, end runs or forward passes are tried. No quarterback worth his salt keeps pounding away with line bucks that yield at best a yard or, worse still, a yardage loss.

The enterprise that engages us is not one against a single restaurant in Atlanta, Ga., or a single school board in Malverne, N.Y., or an employment policy in St. Louis, Mo., or police action in Plaquemine, La., or a single hotel in Salt Lake City, Utah. We are engaged in a comprehensive campaign for the civil rights of 18 million citizens scattered in 50 states, living under varied economic, social and political conditions and functioning with a variety of education and technical knowledge, training and skill.

The 18 millions are a minority in 186 millions of citizens. Thus even elementary reasoning would seem to indicate that allies among the majority must be won and held if the minority's efforts are not to end in frustration and failure. . . .

But uni-racial assaults, brave and dedicated though they may be, which are rooted in one tactic and in no critical appraisal of pertinent factors in a particular encounter, could not only fail in their immediate objective, but could set back the whole civil rights army across the entire action front.

Is it too old-fashioned to suggest that we may need more flexibility in our campaign? . . .

A bulldozer can excavate for a foundation but a block and tackle is required to get a piano into the ninth floor.

Let us not become so inflexible in thought and method that we, too, become vulnerable. . . .

The plain lesson is that we must use every method, every technique, every tool available. We need to devise new tools. Our attack must be across the board and must be leveled at all forms and degrees of second class citizenship. Where one weapon is sufficient, let it be employed. Where a combination is required, let it be used. Where variations in timing and methods will be effective, by all means let us employ these. But let none of us in the North or in the South, "activists" or not, fall into the trap at this crucial stage, of attempting to solve all problems everywhere by a single method.

II

BLACK NATIONALISM

Malcolm X, a former dope peddler and convict, was a member of the separatist Black Muslim religious sect before he decided to form his own "black nationalist" movement in 1964. Cut down by a murderer's bullet in 1965, he became a revered image: the proud, angry black man. His eloquence, passion for justice, and sincerity are evident in the following speech. □ *Malcolm X Speaks*, copyright © 1965 by Merit Publishers and Betty Shabazz. Pp. 31-35, 38-43.

How can you thank a man for giving you what's already yours? How then can you thank him for giving you only part of what's already yours? You haven't even made progress, if what's being given to you, you should have had already. That's not progress. . . .

And now you're facing a situation where the young Negro's coming up. They don't want to hear that "turn-the-other-cheek" stuff, no. In Jacksonville, those were teenagers, they were throwing Molotov cocktails. Negroes have never done that before. But it shows you there's a new deal coming in. There's new thinking coming in. There's new strategy coming in. It'll be Molotov cocktails this month, hand grenades next month, and something else next month. It'll be ballots, or it'll be bullets. It'll be liberty, or it will be death. The only difference about this kind of death — it'll be reciprocal. You know what is meant by "reciprocal"? . . . It takes two to tango; when I go, you go.

. . . Well, we're justified in seeking civil rights, if it means equality of opportunity, because all we're doing there is trying to collect for our investment. Our mothers and fathers invested sweat and blood. Three hundred and ten years we worked in this country without a dime in return — I mean without a *dime* in return. You let the white man walk around here talking about how rich this country is, but you never stop to think how it got rich so quick. It got rich because you made it rich. . . .

This is our investment. This is our contribution — our blood. Not only did we give of our free labor, we gave of our blood. Every time he had a call to arms, we were the first ones in uniform. We died on every battlefield the white man had. We have made a greater sacrifice than anybody who's standing up in America today. We have made a greater contribution and have collected less. Civil rights, for those of us whose philosophy is black nationalism, means: "Give it to us now. Don't wait for next year. Give it to us yesterday, and that's not fast enough." . . .

If you don't take this kind of stand, your little children will grow up and look at you and think "shame." If you don't take an uncompromising stand—I don't mean go out and get violent; but at the same time you should never be nonviolent unless you run into some nonviolence. I'm nonviolent with those who are nonviolent with me. But when you drop that violence on me, then you've made me go insane, and I'm not responsible for what I do. And that's the way every Negro should get. Any time you know you're within the law, within your legal rights, within your moral rights, in accord with justice, then die for what you believe in. But don't die alone. Let your dying be reciprocal. This is what is meant by equality. What's good for the goose is good for the gander.

. . . Uncle Sam's hands are dripping with blood, dripping with the blood of the black man in this country. He's the earth's number-one hypocrite. He has the audacity—yes, he has—imagine him posing as the leader of the free world. The free world!—and you over here singing "We Shall Overcome." Expand the civil-rights struggle to the level of human rights, take it into the United Nations, where our African brothers can throw their weight on our side, where our Asian brothers can throw their weight on our side, where our Latin-American brothers can throw their weight on our side, and where 800 million Chinamen are sitting there waiting to throw their weight on our side.

Let the world know how bloody his hands are. Let the world know the hypocrisy that's practiced over here. Let it be the ballot or the bullet. Let him know that it must be the ballot or the bullet. . . .

The political philosophy of black nationalism means that the black man should control the politics and the politicians in his own community; no more. The black man in the black community has to be re-educated into the science of politics so he will know what politics is supposed to bring him in return. Don't be throwing out any ballots. A ballot is like a bullet. You don't throw your ballots until you see a target, and if that target is not within your reach, keep your ballot in your pocket. The political philosophy of black nationalism is being taught in the Christian church. It's being taught in the NAACP. It's being taught in CORE meetings. It's being taught in SNCC [Student Nonviolent Coordinating Committee] meetings. It's being taught in Muslim meetings. It's being taught where nothing but atheists and agnostics come together. It's being taught everywhere. Black people are fed up with the dillydallying, pussyfooting, compromising approach that we've been using toward getting our freedom. We want freedom *now*, but we're not going to get it saying "We Shall Overcome." We've got to fight until we overcome.

The economic philosophy of black nationalism is pure and simple. It only means that we should control the economy of our community. Why should white people be running all the stores in our community? Why should white people be running the banks of our community? Why should the economy of our community be in the hands of the white man? Why? If a black man can't move his store into a white community, you tell me why a white man should move his store into a black community. . . . [The] white man has got all our stores in the community tied up; so that though we spend it in the community, at sundown the man who runs the store takes it over across town somewhere. He's got us in a vise.

So the economic philosophy of black nationalism means in every church, in every civic organization, in every fraternal order, it's time now for our people to become conscious of the importance of controlling the economy of our community. If we own the stores, if we operate the businesses, if we try and establish some industry in our own community, then we're developing to the position where we are creating employment for our own kind. Once you gain control of the economy of your own community, then you don't have to picket and boycott and beg some cracker [white] downtown for a job in his business.

The social philosophy of black nationalism only means that we have to get together and remove the evils, the vices, alcoholism, drug addiction, and other evils that are destroying the moral fiber of our community. We ourselves have to lift the level of our community, the standard of our community to a higher level, make our own society beautiful so that we will be satisfied in our own social circles and won't be running around here trying to knock our way into a social circle where we're not wanted. . . .

I have watched how Billy Graham comes into a city, spreading what he calls the gospel of Christ, which is only white nationalism. That's what he is. Billy Graham is a white nationalist; I'm a black nationalist. . . .

Our gospel is black nationalism. We're not trying to threaten the existence of any organization, but we're spreading the gospel of black nationalism. Anywhere there's a church that is also preaching and practicing the gospel of black nationalism, join that church. If the NAACP is preaching and practicing the gospel of black nationalism, join the NAACP. If CORE is spreading and practicing the gospel of black nationalism, join CORE. Join any organization that has a gospel that's for the uplift of the black man. And when you get into it and see them pussyfooting or compromising, pull out of it because that's not black nationalism. We'll find another one. . . .

It's time for you and me to stop sitting in this country, letting some cracker senators, Northern crackers and Southern crackers, sit there in Washington, D.C., and come to a conclusion in their mind that you and I are supposed to have civil rights. There's no white man going to tell me anything about *my* rights. . . . You let that white man know, if this is a country of freedom, let it be a country of freedom; and if it's not a country of freedom, change it. . . .

Last but not least, I must say this concerning the great controversy over rifles and shotguns. The only thing that I've ever said is that in areas where the government has proven itself either unwilling or unable to defend the lives and the property of Negroes, it's time for Negroes to defend themselves. . . . If the white man doesn't want the black man buying rifles and shotguns, then let the government do its job. That's all.

III

THE BLACK PANTHER PROGRAM

The Black Panther Party, a controversial organization, had a reputation for extremist views. The Party's program, as outlined in its newspaper, is a combination of black nationalism, socialism, and demands for better conditions for Negroes. □ Abridgement from "What We Want, What We Believe," *The Black Panther*, June 27, 1970, page 21. Reprinted with permission of the Black Panther Party.

1. We want freedom. We want power to determine the destiny of our Black Community. . . .

2. We want full employment for our people. We believe that the federal government is responsible and obligated to give every man employment or a guaranteed income. We believe that if the white

American businessmen will not give full employment, then the means of production should be taken from the businessmen and placed in the community so that the people of the community can organize and employ all of its people and give a high standard of living.

3. We want an end to the robbery by the CAPITALIST of our Black Community. We believe that this racist government has robbed us and now we are demanding the overdue debt of forty acres and two mules. Forty acres and two mules was promised 100 years ago as restitution for slave labor and mass murder of black people. We will accept the payment in currency which will be distributed to our many communities. . . .

4. We want decent housing, fit for shelter of human beings. We believe that if the white landlords will not give decent housing to our black community, then the housing and the land should be made into cooperatives so that our community, with government aid, can build and make decent housing for its people.

5. We want education for our people that exposes the true nature of this decadent American society. We want education that teaches us our true history and our role in the present-day society. . . .

6. We want all black men to be exempt from military service. We believe that Black people should not be forced to fight in the military service to defend a racist government that does not protect us. We will not fight and kill other people of color in the world who, like black people, are being victimized by the white racist government of America. We will protect ourselves from the force and violence of the racist police and the racist military, by whatever means necessary.

7. We want an immediate end to POLICE BRUTALITY and MURDER of black people. We believe we can end police brutality in our black community by organizing black self-defense groups that are dedicated to defending our black community from racist police oppression and brutality. The Second Amendment to the Constitution of the United States gives a right to bear arms. We therefore believe that all black people should arm themselves for self-defense.

8. We want freedom for all black men held in federal, state, county and city prisons and jails. We believe that all black people should be released from the many jails and prisons because they have not received a fair and impartial trial.

9. We want all black people when brought to trial to be tried in court by a jury of their peer group or people from their black communities, as defined by the Constitution of the United States. . . .

10. We want land, bread, housing, education, clothing, justice and peace. And as our major political objective, a United Nations-supervised plebiscite to be held throughout the black colony in which only black colonial subjects will be allowed to participate, for the purpose of determining the will of black people as to their national destiny.

[The first part of the American Declaration of Independence, as quoted in the selection, follows.]

When, in the course of human events, it becomes necessary for one people to dissolve the political bands which have connected them with another, and to assume, among the powers of the earth, the separate and equal station to which the laws of nature and nature's God entitle them, a decent respect to the opinions of mankind requires that they should declare the causes which impel them to the separation.

We hold these truths to be self-evident, that all men are created equal; that they are endowed by their Creator with certain unalienable rights; that among these are life, liberty, and the pursuit of happiness. That, to secure these rights, governments are instituted among men, deriving their just powers from the consent of the governed; that, whenever any form of government becomes destructive of these ends, it is the right of the people to alter or to abolish it, and to institute a new government, laying its foundation on such principles, and organizing its powers in such form, as to them shall seem most likely to effect their safety and happiness. Prudence, indeed, will dictate that governments long established should not be changed for light and transient causes; and, accordingly, all experience hath shown, that mankind are more disposed to suffer, while evils are sufferable, than to right themselves by abolishing the forms to which they are accustomed. **But, when a long train of abuses and usurpations, pursuing invariably the same object, evinces a design to reduce them under absolute despotism, it is their right, it is their duty, to throw off such government, and to provide new guards for their future security.**

IV

WHO SPEAKS FOR THE BLACK AMERICAN?

In 1969, *Time* magazine analyzed the positions of various black leaders. ☐ Abridgement of "The Future of Black Leadership" from *Time* (April 4, 1969). Reprinted by permission from *Time*, The Weekly Newsmagazine; Copyright Time Inc., 1969. Pp. 29–30.

It is a year since Martin Luther King, Jr. died. Who speaks for the black American now?

The question itself irritates Negroes. Who, they respond, speaks for the white American? Is it Richard Nixon, who gained the presidency with only 43.4% of the popular vote? George Wallace, who achieved more ballots than any other third-party candidate in the nation's history? If, as one magazine recently claimed, Singer James Brown, "Soul Brother No. 1," is the most powerful Afro-American, who is the most powerful Italian-American? Frank Sinatra?

White America is only now beginning to understand the diversity of Negro society. That dawning recognition may be a hopeful sign. Instead of racial discrimination, it might mean human discrimination, a capacity to distinguish among the enormously varied aspects of black America. Says the National Urban League's Whitney Young: "Somehow the white community has got to get over the idea that we should provide them with a black messiah who will be all things to all men. Whites seem to be able to distinguish their own crackpots from the rest, but when there's a riot of blacks, it's all just blacks.". . .

It is impossible to know what King—and another assassinated black leader, Malcolm X . . . —might have done to change the struggle, had they lived. According to King's assistant, Wyatt Tee Walker: "Their deaths set back our struggle by 25 years." Even toward the end of King's life, however, he may have suspected that he was losing his constituency among blacks because of the change in Negro psychology. The thrust of the nonviolent crusade had been integration of schools and public facilities, voting rights and new civil rights laws. Yet the brutal circumstances of life remained. Frustration grew. King's following soured. He was hooted in Watts when he preached nonviolence a day after the riots in 1965. His open-occupancy reform campaign in Chicago failed. The Memphis garbage strike seemed his last hope to redeem his philosophy. . . .

A Harris poll last year [1968] recorded that 92% of black students, including the most militant, still favor integration. Separatism is perhaps a demand for the creation of an Africa of the mind more than a bid for a geographical republic. If literally fulfilled, black nationalism might be disastrous. Negroes are beginning to realize that even the admirable notion of black capitalism is futile unless joined to white capitalism, to the U.S. economy outside the ghettos. . . . Separatism might incite rampage and also tragically alienate the Negro middle class, which has more in common with the white middle class than with the black poor.

. . . Black leadership now appears without direction. Whitney Young remains one of the two or three most influential black leaders, but many Negroes feel that he is trying to satisfy all factions. Roy Wilkins, despite the 450,000 membership of the N.A.A.C.P., has lost more ground than any other leader, with the decline of integration as the principal issue and the loss of the N.A.A.C.P.'s traditional adversary role. To be sure, the constituencies of older Negro activists are underestimated, especially in a press that publicizes the shocking more often than quiet accomplishment. "Some leaders," says Young, "are followed by seven Negroes and 70 screaming reporters." On the other hand, if many blacks remain personally conservative, they also welcome flamboyant gestures. . . .

. . . [There] are younger black leaders . . . : Georgia State Legislator Julian Bond, 29, bridges the gap between moderates and extremists, middle and lower classes, old and young. Chicago's Rev. Jesse Jackson, 27, with his "Operation Breadbasket," coercing local merchants to hire Negroes, has, some Negroes think, an overweening ambition. But, says Bond, "what we need is 150 Jesse Jacksons."

Such leaders plainly have national potential. But for the present, black Americans are suspicious of figures who have been either . . . [praised or blamed] by the national press . . . . The fact is that black leaders are proliferating, mostly on the local level and without the white man's cachet [stamp of approval] — a most significant development. Even black women are becoming more politically effective — as with Mississippi's Fannie Lou Hamer, [and] Brooklyn Congresswoman Shirley Chisholm . . . . Says Dr. Nathan Wright, an early organizer of Black Power conferences: "The old idea of controlling Negroes through Negro leaders is finished. We need technicians and facilitators."

The new emphasis on local leadership has caused trouble, including bitter feuds and even murders. Scores of ambitious men are vying to represent black communities across the country, but few have yet learned the arts of political compromise. In some ways, the toughest job in America now is being the black mayor of a white city — not because of white hostility but because black radicals scorn such officials for allegedly selling out. . . .

In 1966, Martin Luther King said: "I don't think that anything can be more tragic in the civil rights movement than the attitude that the black man can solve his problems by himself." Indeed, Cleveland's Mayor Carl Stokes and Gary's Mayor Richard Hatcher could not have been elected without considerable white support. White cooperation is vital at every level of development, if only because . . . [of] the basic ratio of blacks to whites in the U.S. population. . . .

Today the majority of Negroes probably . . . wish to consolidate their own turf and then decide on what terms they will participate in the larger American society. Tomorrow may bring more strife — or peaceful racial pride. Whatever the outcome, more and more local black leaders are bent on building black establishments and seeing that no one, black or white, burns them down. White Americans are well advised to provide every ounce of help they can.

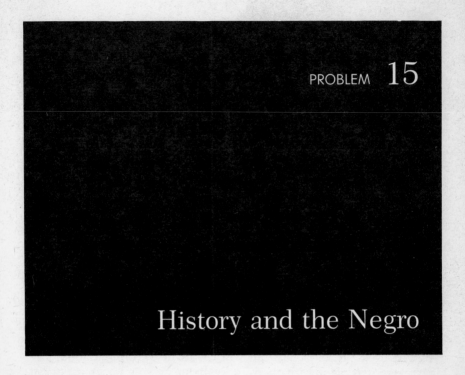

PROBLEM 15

History and the Negro

"The trouble is that the history of the world has been distorted. White people have given it to us and like fools we've swallowed it, hook, line and sinker. . . .

"The trouble with the white world is that nothing is discovered until they set foot on it. Now dig. If they tell you Columbus discovered America in 1492, you'd say, yes, he did. Look how silly you are. When they came here there was already people here, but they don't recognize anybody who's not white."

These remarks were made in 1967 by Stokely Carmichael. A former integrationist, he became convinced that all the efforts of the black community should be directed at getting itself together rather than integrating with white America. Militants like Carmichael waved the banner of black pride and used every opportunity to emphasize that white Americans were to blame for the impoverished conditions in black ghettos. Their angry words reflected a deep look into the psychological aspects of slavery and Jim Crow. According to their reasoning, these two institutions had stamped a feeling of inferiority upon Negroes, shame that had to be replaced by a sense of pride.

In particular, angry young Negroes attacked another form of prejudice — Jim Crow history. They felt that white historians had, over the years, ignored the accomplishments of black people. Thus, Negroes who had performed herioc deeds or had been successful statesmen or had invented important devices were left out of most history books.

Such complaints had significant influence on historical writing and research and, especially, on educational materials in the late 1960's. Historians began to write about the early black African kingdoms and to emphasize the contributions of Negro citizens to American society. A flood of materials was made available for the nation's classrooms in both white suburbs and black ghettos.

As the search to rediscover Negro heroes gained momentum, some historians and educators felt that it could go too far; that unworthy men might be given undue praise just because their skins had been black; that Negro militants could prove to be just as guilty of distorting history as the books that ignored Negroes. The debate concerning history and the Negro centered on how best to integrate Jim Crow history. The selections in this Problem analyze different answers to this question.

As you read, think about these questions:

1   Do you think Carmichael's statements (Reading I) about George Washington and Abraham Lincoln are true? Why?

2   What is the difference between "Black History" and "Negro History" according to Cuban? Why does Cuban believe that "Black History" has no place in the public schools? Why does Banks disagree with Cuban on this point? With whom do you agree?

3   In what ways, if any, do the three selections agree?

4   Is this book "Black History," "Negro History," or "White History"? Explain your answer.

5   What connections are there between the selections in Problem 10, which dealt with the 1920's, and this Problem?

I

A MILITANT VIEWPOINT

In this speech (which was also quoted in the introduction) Stokely Carmichael urges his all-black audience to have pride in their race and to substitute black heroes for the white men praised in their history books. ☐ Abridgement of Stokely Carmichael's speech at Ebenezer Baptist Church on Thursday, March 2, 1967 from *Pittsburgh Point* (March 9, 1967). Reprinted by permission of The Pittsburgh Point. P. 6.

Some people may not like the truth. But the truth is the salvation of black people today. You can't run from it. You've got to embrace it. And I'm here to tell the truth about black people and this country today.

This country has always told *lies* about us. White people believe those lies, and what's bad is that some black people believe those lies too. (applause) . . .

. . . [Some] Negroes say, "the trouble is all black. Anything all black is bad." You ought to understand that very carefully. You're talking about yourself because you're black from the bottom of your feet to the nappy hair on the top of your head. You ought not to be saying anything all black is bad. You ought to say anything black is good, it's good! (cheers)

Anybody who'll tell you he's a successful *Neeeeegro* (laughter), the first thing he says is that he moved out of the ghetto from *those* people. (applause) Now that's their success that they've moved away from black people because we hate each other so much that all our lives we try to be white ("that's right, that's right!")

We hate it so much we try to look white. Because the white people say that in order to be beautiful one has to have thin lips, thin nose and stringy hair. (laughter-cheers) That's right, that's what they say. Black people all their lives try to do that.

They get up their matting-over [whitening] cream. (cheers-foot stamping)

Not even satisfied with that they wear wigs to cover up their hair. (cheers, laughter)

You see our children on buses holding their noses so they won't come open. (laughter-cheers)

My mother didn't want me to drink coffee because it would make me black. You know your mothers said the same thing to you. (more laughter and cheers)

I want you to understand now this country has worked on our minds. . . .

What we have to recognize is that white and black is different. White people have thin lips, thin noses and stringy hair. We are black. We have broad noses, thick lips, and nappy hair. We are black, and we are beautiful, (cheers) and we are beautiful! (more cheers)

. . .You've got to understand the job of educating black people lies with us, not white people. They can't educate us. (applause) We have to begin to educate ourselves, because hating black in this country goes very deep. . . .

Now when we're ready to rewrite the history of this nation, we'll say this nation is a nation of thieves ("That's right") It stole the United States from the Indians, and wasn't satisfied, killed practically every last one of 'em. But not only were those crackers [white men] not satisfied with stealing the Indians and the land, they turned around and stole us from Africa. They started it by calling this the land of the free and the home of the brave, and that's the history we're supposed to follow. And you here talkin' about "My country 'tis of thee." . . .

We have to be crystal clear in our minds when we move for our liberation this time around, because this man is not playing with us. And we got to be prepared, 'cause if you think [President] Johnson is talking about crime in the street, he's talking about stopping us. I don't care how nice he makes it sound. When he talks about riot equipment, you know who he talkin' about. And if we don't make up our minds, we going to be like the Jewish people in Germany in the nineteen thirties. (applause)

They only let us respect people who died for their liberation. Have you dug that? They hold up George Washington Carver. Well they need him, because without him white folks would be eating only jelly sandwiches. (applause-cheers) They hold up Booker T. Washington for us.

That means we have to get our own heroes for our children. We can't let them give us heroes any more. Little kid up there talking about George Washington never cut down a cherry tree. You know that cracker sold a black woman for a barrel of molasses? (cheers) What you talkin' about George Washington? You know he denied our existence. How can we call him our hero? He had slaves and sold one of us for a barrel of molasses. And he's their founding father. And you want to know why this country is so full of racism.

And then they hold up Abraham Lincoln. Our hero, Abraham Lincoln. He freed us. You dig him? He freed us, and he didn't free us until 1863, when the war started in 1861. Because the South was winning—that's why he freed us. The slaves were doing labor and let the Southerners free to kill people in the North, and when Lincoln understood it, that's when he freed the slaves. And not only that—when he freed us, he wouldn't let us fight. We weren't fit to fight for our own freedom. Do you know about a great black man named Frederick Douglas [sic]? Did you know that it was Frederick Douglas [sic] went and straightened that cracker out and told him he better let us fight for our own liberation? Lincoln was getting ready to ship you back to Africa, lock, stock and barrel. He was a leading exponent of the colonization theory. Abraham Lincoln—and he freed us. You dig that?

We will pick our heroes. They will be the Denmark Veseys. He burnt up all the white folks' crops during slavery time. He started a slave revolt and burnt the crops to the ground and killed every white man in his way 'cause they were keeping him in slavery and it's honorable to fight for your liberation. Dig it?

We will raise up to W. E. B. DuBois, who understood what was happening in this country a long time ago. We will raise up to Marcus Garvey, for teaching us pride in our race. We will hold close to the Richard Wrights, and we will make Malcolm X our leader. (applause)

We must give our youth the spirit to fight. This country started off when it said "Give me liberty or give me death."

II

BLACK HISTORY, NEGRO HISTORY, AND WHITE FOLK

In this selection, it is claimed that there are two forms of history that can, and should, be taught to black children. The author (who is also the author of this book) is a teacher in the Washington, D.C., public schools. ☐ "Black History, Negro History, and White Folk" by Larry Cuban from *Saturday Review* (September 21, 1968). Copyright © 1968 Saturday Review, Inc. Reprinted by permission of Saturday Review, Inc. Pp. 64-65.

Booker T. Washington is an Uncle Tom; Nat Turner is a Freedom Fighter; Abraham Lincoln is a white supremacist, and the first President of the United States is just another honkie. Mali, Songhay, and Timbuktu [of African history] are enshrined, and hog maws, chittlings, and black-eyed peas are ennobled. This is the stuff of Black History. Heroes are all black and struggle for freedom. Villains are all white and oppress for profit. Black History, a tool in the hands of race-conscious activists who wish to create a sense of people – ness among black people, bursts with righteousness, pride, and outrage.

Negro History, on the other hand, corrects distortions and fills in the enormous gaps of information about people of color in this nation. Restraint and balance mark this approach; injustice is soberly catalogued. Colored inventors, soldiers, and artists enter their proper chronological niches and tell Americans that this country is indebted to the invisible man. A history unit on the westward movement, for instance, includes adequate treatment in text and pictures of Jim Beckworth (fur trapper), Nat Love (Deadwood Dick of the 1880s), and the Indian pacification efforts of the Ninth and Tenth Cavalry units.

Negro History, in short, speaks to the mind of the white man and to the middle- and upper-income Negro over thirty-five. Black History speaks to the soul of black men, especially the young.

The distinction, of course, is not absolute. But the differences in style, content, and audience between the two histories have crystallized sufficiently in recent years to become clear. Indeed the split over aims and audiences mirror the larger conflicts over the whys and wherefores of race consciousness.

Consider the recent flood of books and materials on the Negro. Much criticism has been directed at books that glorify such individuals as Crispus Attucks, who is, at best, a shadowy historical figure. What critics fail to realize is that such materials are part of a determined effort to counter the white propaganda that has blanketed public schools since their inception. In the process, such materials create a pantheon of black heroes that children can point to with pride. Movements need heroes – martyrs, preferably – and Attucks, Nat Turner, and Malcolm X can be used to convince black people that they counted years ago and they count now.

To evaluate a book on Attucks solely by the canons of scholarly objectivity and historical accuracy is missing the point – it ignores the necessity of creating black counterparts to the Nathan Hales and Molly Pitchers of the white past. That equally shadowy white heroes have been manufactured in the name of patriotism should give pause to those critics who attack such books without considering their purpose or audience.

The basic issue is whether black mythology will compete with white mythology – commonly called "social studies" – or whether mythology, black or white, belongs in the public schools at all.

To the proponents of Negro History there seem to be three main purposes which competent, well trained teachers can hope to achieve: 1) offer Negro and white students a more balanced picture of the American past, 2) improve racial relations, and 3) improve the self-concept of Negro children. Black History advocates accept the first, care little if at all for the second, and emphasize the third most strongly. Pride, dignity, and self-respect are the vocabulary of Black History.

This poses the question of whether studying Negro or Black History actually will improve the self-concept and instill pride. The only answer has to be: No one knows. No evidence has been produced to demonstrate whether children will see themselves and their race in a more positive light as a result of instructional materials or a course in high school. That no evidence exists, of course, does not mean that increased self-esteem and pride are not produced. But it is clear that creating a course or writing a book for the express purpose of instilling racial pride requires a selection of content that stresses only the positive, only the success story, only the hero, only the victory. And this is propaganda. I don't know whether it works, but I do know that its place is in the storefront, not the classroom. Its teacher must be a true believer, not an inquirer; and it can only be taught by a race-conscious black man, not a white man.

Within the framework of a public school, the only legitimate goals for ethnic content that can be achieved are to offer a balanced view of the American past and present, including racism and democratic ideals, and to equip students with the skills to analyze the meaning of the black American's experience in this country. Whether this combination of knowledge and analytical skills will raise self-esteem or invest youngsters with dignity is debatable, but both could help students to know and think about the many dimensions of the American experience, free of propaganda.

But the activists are dissatisfied with "integrated" history—and with some reason. Most efforts to incorporate the role of the Negro into the course of study simply haven't worked because of the fear, unwillingness, and ignorance of teachers and administrators, both black and white. Consider Washington, D.C., where 80 per cent of the schoolteachers are Negro. In 1964, the Board of Education published a curriculum guide on Negro history for teachers that corrected the distortions and omissions. Yet in visiting classrooms in the District, one finds a tiny fraction of the teachers using the guide, and a majority seldom even incorporate ethnic materials into the conventional content. School people must learn what black activists already know—it is not the materials but the teacher that makes the difference.

When we turn to the contrasting opinions over who should teach history to black children, the answers seem deceptively clear. To most Negroes and whites the answer hinges upon the academic training and competency of the teacher, regardless of race. To Black History advocates, concerned less with the facts than with redefining blackness in a positive manner, only a black man can teach the subject. But the first point of view fails to accept the reality of experience, and the second advocates a kind of educational apartheid [segregation] that inflates skin color to the single most important variable in teaching—which it isn't.

On his pilgrimage to Mecca in 1964, Malcolm X discovered that he could break bread with a blond, blue-eyed Moslem and be treated as a brother; the trip convinced him that skin color is less important than point of view. Awareness, not pigment, is crucial. Black students learn the same thing when they discover that many of their Negro teachers care little for the issues that confront youth today. And it is doubly galling when they see a young white teacher who is not afraid to raise issues of racial conflict, protest movements, and poverty. Bitterly, they wonder who exactly is "white" and who is "black."

Less attention should be paid to additional books and courses, then, and more to the craftsman who will use the tools. Preachers of Black History know that the person is far more important than the materials he uses. Advocates of Negro History have yet to learn this. There is much to be learned about teaching and learning from the unorthodox, intuitional growth of the Black History movement. But only so much.

Black History aims at revitalizing the African heritage, specifying white racism and the race's liberation from it, and defining a positive black culture—all of which is geared to producing a proud people capable of initiating basic changes in society. It is necessary. It should be supported. But it belongs . . . outside the public schools. It belongs in the after-school classes established by CORE and the NAACP in Cleveland, the private schools created by Black Muslims in Chicago and other cities, and in the many storefront classes developed by Afro-American societies across the country.

The movement is a growing, vital force capturing the imagination and soul of black youth. If Black History can recruit youngsters and instill in them a passionate race consciousness, the public schools will benefit from youth who know themselves and are committed to use education to shape their future in this country. Not fear but support is essential for after-school centers, cultural exhibitions, and private schools. Fear becomes an issue, however, when Black History becomes the pretext for the thrust toward black control of schools where the goals of public education become unraveled by the search for a political power base.

And Negro History? Its place is in the public schools. It is essential to the growth of both black and white students. Borrowing some of the content, approach, and emphasis of Black History, effective teachers of Negro History, of either race, can begin the enormous task of eliminating the white mythology that has dominated the public schools for too long. The two histories, Black and Negro, need not strain against one another. Rather they can mesh gears and begin moving Americans toward an examination of themselves and their past. Something this country needs badly.

III

THE NATURE OF HISTORY

Cuban's ideas were challenged by James A. Banks, an education professor at the University of Washington. He noted that all historians are biased in one way or another. □ James A. Banks, A Letter to the Editor ("Varieties of History"), *Harvard Educational Review*, 39, Winter 1969, 155-158. Copyright © 1969 by President and Fellows of Harvard College.

. . . [A] growing number of white "liberal" educators . . . are alarmed by what they perceive as attempts by black militants to "distort" history by glorifying the black man's past in order to imbue pride in black students. . . .

Cuban . . . [and other educators] err when they assume that there is such a phenomenon as unbiased, objective, and balanced written history. . . . [They] believe that the historian, by carefully gathering data, can derive historical statements which are balanced, factual and without distortions. This assumption emanates from a confusion of *historical facts* with *past events*. . . . [The educators] imply that historical facts are hard and stable, waiting to be uncovered by the studious, objective historian. . . . [The] historian can never deal with actual past events, but must deal with *statements about events* written by biased individuals with divergent points of view. Moreover, the historian necessarily and inevitably reflects his own biases in his attempts to reconstruct the past. Using various sources to find out about past events, the historian *must* select from the statements which he uncovers those which he wishes to report and to regard as factual. The historian can never discover all the "facts" about a past event; his selection and interpretation are greatly influenced by his personal bias, cultural environment and his reasons for writing. . . .

We cannot . . . contend that any versions of history are "balanced" and without distortions, because historical facts are products of the human mind and are not identical with past events. The most we can say about any version of history is that its statements are regarded as factual by a greater number of historians than other statements which comprise other varieties of history. The versions of history accepted as most factual by historians vary greatly with the times, the culture, and the discovery of artifacts and documents. The present heavily influences how historians view the past. . . .

Implicit in Cuban's argument is the belief that statements which constitute Negro History are more widely regarded as factual by white, liberal historians than the statements which constitute Black History. He assumes that because these statements are more widely accepted by "established" white historians they more accurately describe past events than statements which constitute Black History. . . . We cannot accept consensus within the community of white, established historians as adequate evidence for historical accuracy. This is true not only because there is rarely agreement among historians on controversial issues, but because historians in different countries and in different times regard highly conflicting statements as factual. . . .

The writers of Negro History attempt to construct history which reflects the opinions of established historians (most of whom are white); writers of Black History write history primarily to imbue pride in black students; writers of white schoolbook history write to glorify the United States and to develop patriotism in white children. Because of the tenuous nature of history, we are more justified in questioning the aims of these different varieties of history than we are in challenging the accuracy of the statements which they promulgate. Since black people are vehemently complaining about the treatment of the Negro in schoolbooks, which were written by white established historians and educators, we cannot assume that the professional white historian has fewer biases than the black militant historian.

Cuban . . . and other educators . . . grossly misinterpret the proper role of history in the public school. These educators assume that there is an "accurate" version of history, and that it is the role of the teacher to help youngsters become effective consumers of this authentic and balanced history. Actually, the role of the school . . . is to help students ". . . create their own accounts of the past and to pit their conclusions against those of other writers of history." . . . [By] approaching the study of history in this way, students will realize that there are alternative ways of looking at identical events and situations; consequently, their reasoning and critical powers will be strengthened.

In writing their own accounts of history, students should determine for themselves which versions of history are more accurate and balanced. *To do this, they must be exposed to all types and varieties of history, including Negro History, Black History and White Schoolbook History.* Students should also be exposed to different versions of history because thinking occurs when students are forced to consider conflicting interpretations and points of view. To ban any version of history from the public school is to deny the student academic freedom. Students should not have to go to the storefront school to encounter versions of history which conflict with *the* version endorsed by established institutions.

By reading historical documents, examining historical artifacts, reading accounts of history written by others, and writing their own versions of history, students will discover that written history is at best accounts of events from particular points of view. The conclusions which students derive about the accuracy of historical statements, and the versions of history which they construct will be greatly influenced by their own personal biases and cultural environment. We cannot confiscate the student's right to reach his own conclusions regarding the accuracy of historical statements and to construct his own accounts of history. Rather, we should encourage students to carefully consider all points of view and to responsibly defend their own judgments. . . . [For] the ultimate goal of social education is to help students develop a commitment to inquiry and not to make them unthinking consumers of any version of history.